WIN WORK POLITICS AS A LEADER

By

Marc White

Disclaimer

Foreword

First, I would like to thank you for taking the first step of trusting
me and deciding to purchase/read this life-transforming eBook.
Thanks for spending your time and resources on this material.

I can assure you of exact results if you will diligently follow the
exact blueprint, I lay bare in the information manual you are cur-
rently reading. It has transformed lives, and I strongly believe it
will equally transform your own life too.

Acknowledgments

Writing a book is harder than I thought and more rewarding than I could have ever imagined. None of this would have been possible without the blessings of God.

I would like to thank my family and friends who supported and encouraged me for writing this book. My sincere thanks to all of you.

The world is a better place thanks to people who want to develop and lead others. What makes it even better are people who share the gift of their time to mentor future leaders. Thank you to everyone who strives to grow and help others grow.

Without the experiences and support from my peers and teams, this book would not exist.

INTRODUCTION

Workplace politics is the process and behavior in human interactions involving power and authority. It is also a tool to assess the operational capacity and to balance diverse views of interested parties. It is also known as office politics and organizational politics. It is the use of power and social networking within an organization to achieve changes that benefit the organization or individuals within it.

Organizational politics are self-serving behaviors that employees use to increase the probability of obtaining positive outcomes in organizations. Influence by individuals may serve personal interests without regard to their effect on the organization itself. Some of the personal advantages may include access to tangible assets or intangible benefits such as status or pseudo-authority that influences the behavior of others. Positive politics are behaviors that are designed to influence others to help both the organization and the person playing the politics. Examples of positive politics include portraying a professional image, publicizing one's accomplishments, volunteering, and complimenting others.

On the other hand, organizational politics can increase efficiency, form interpersonal relationships, expedite change, and profit the organization and its members simultaneously. Both individuals and groups may engage in office politics which can be highly destructive, as people focus on personal gains at the expense of the organization. Self-serving political actions can negatively influence our social groupings, cooperation, information sharing, and many other organizational functions. Thus, it is vital to pay attention to organizational politics and create the right political landscape. Negative politics are designed to achieve personal gain at the expense of others and the organization. Examples of negative politics are spreading rumors, talking behind someone's back, and not telling someone important information.

Politics is the lubricant that oils your organization's internal gears. Office politics has also been described as merely how power gets worked out on a practical, day-to-day basis.

In scientific research, human behavior is a complex interplay of three components: actions, cognition, and emotions.

Sounds complicated? Let's address them one by one.

Action

An action denotes everything that can be observed, either with bare eyes or measured by physiological sensors. Think of action as an initiation or transition from one state to another – at a movie set, the director shouts "action" for the next scene to be filmed.

Behavioral actions can take place on various time scales, ranging from muscular activation to sweat gland activity, food consumption, or sleep.

Cognition

Cognitions describe thoughts and mental images you carry with you, and they can be both verbal and nonverbal. "I have to remember to buy groceries," or "I'd be curious to know what she thinks of me," can be considered verbal cognitions. In contrast, imagine how your house will look like after remodeling could be regarded as a nonverbal cognition.

Cognitions comprise skills and knowledge – knowing how to use tools in a meaningful manner (without hurting yourself).

Emotion

Commonly, an emotion is any relatively brief conscious experience characterized by intense mental activity and a feeling that is not described as resulting from either reasoning or knowledge. This usually exists on a scale, from positive (pleasurable) to negative (unpleasant).

Other aspects of physiology that are indicative of emotional processing – such as increased heart rate or respiration rate caused by increased arousal are usually hidden to the eye. Similar to cognitions, emotions cannot be observed directly. They can only be inferred indirectly by tracking facial electromyographic activity

Actions, cognitions, and emotions do not run independently of each other – their proper interaction enables you to perceive the world around you, listen to your inner wishes and respond appropriately to people in your surroundings. However, it is hard to tell what exactly is cause and effect – turning your head (action) and seeing a familiar face might cause a sudden burst of joy (emotion) accompanied by an internal realization (cognition).

PRODUCTIVE APPROACH TO NAVIGATE WORK POLITICS

Give Voice To The Problem

When workplace drama affects you, it can become an insidious cloud that permeates your day-to-day. As long as it remains nebulous, it will continue to impact your focus and productivity negatively. Take back control by giving this cloud a name and making it concrete. Be mindful and ask yourself, "What is going on here?" Focus on the facts and avoid what you think happened. Know that you can't control how you feel, only how you react. This will make future conversations easier.

Count Your Elephants

Make a list of all of the elephants in the room. These are the awkward, uncomfortable realities that haven't been discussed out in the open. Set aside time to consciously think through what's bothering you right now and write down these elephants. This will not only enable you to resolve these issues but will also give you peace of mind.

Identify Your Role In The Problem

Be honest with yourself: Are you contributing to the situation negatively or doing anything to help? Even if you're only contributing 5%, that's 5% you have direct power over. Write down how you've contributed and identified how you can personally take responsibility. If you do this authentically, it will be your secret weapon to get "opponents" to open up and work with you.

Find The Key Player(s)

In some situations, there is one person at the source of the problem. Go through all the players and imagine each person individually disappearing from the organization. Does the problem go away? If it does, then this person is the key. If this person's performance is the issue, that's the elephant in the room that you need to address tactfully. For any other issue, your best weapon is to find empathy for this person. Seek to understand their motivation, and you may find a natural way to diffuse the situation.

Free Yourself From The Ally Echo-Chamber

You know your allies, as you've likely been venting to them. But they are red herrings that may be making things worse, as the venting reduces the symptoms just enough to keep everyone from addressing the core problem. They can also distort reality by allowing you to focus on your own version of what happened instead of the facts. Don't give in to this distraction.

Identify Your Opponents And Establish A Connection With Them

Empathy diffuses drama. Seek to understand their emotions and what they're trying to accomplish. When you show genuine compassion to your detractors and opponents, it can completely shift the conversation. Even if your opinion is unchanged, a true connection is your greatest asset to influence someone for the better.

Order Conversations From Most Difficult To Least, Then Have Them In That Order

If a conversation feels like it will be difficult, it means it's the most important one to stop avoiding. If you come to the table taking responsibility, seeking empathy, and using as much tact as you can muster, you'll find that even if you disagree, you'll have a useful, productive conversation.

Intentionally Make Yourself Vulnerable

When starting an awkward conversation, lead with what you could have done better in the situation and consider sharing your emotions and challenges in a tactful, authentic way. This is a huge opportunity to create trust. It's also where most people fail, as it requires being incredibly vulnerable. If you're not used to it, force yourself, and the more you do it, the easier it will get. Eventually, as I have found, it will become second nature.

Tactfully Reveal The Elephants

Once you've shared your role in the problem, it's time to discuss the undiscussed. Tell the story of what you think happened, doing your best to reveal the humanity and emotions of every individual that took part. A well-constructed narrative can generate oxytocin "the trust chemical" in the brain of the listener. Be mindful of using language that does not assign judgment or cause people to feel blamed. Instead, focus on the challenges you have been encountering and use neutral language to share your perspective. Your words will only be heard if you are incredibly tactful. It doesn't hurt to practice with a trusted friend!

Prevent Problems By Quickly Addressing Minor Peeves And Triggers

A good roommate knows that the best way to maintain a drama-free home is to share quickly and tactfully when small issues come up. Even though each chat may be a bit awkward, if you come from a place of honesty, identifying where you've been inauthentic or not holding up your end of the bargain, you'll maintain an open dialog. This is the best way to prevent drama and politics from even occurring.

Many of these steps indeed require empathy, rigorous honesty, and vulnerability. They are, however, how high-trust companies are built and maintained. Research shows that they lead to better energy, productivity, engagement, life satisfaction and more. I've found this to be the case at my tech company, and my journey to get here has been incredibly rewarding for myself and those I work with.

OPEN/OVERT BEHAVIORS

Overt behavior refers to actions that can be observed. These include behaviors such as whispering, walking, yawning, and jumping. People who study human behavior sometimes classify overt actions by form, intensity, duration, and frequency.

For instance, walking potentially fits into many possible classifications. One example of walking is a stooped form, an intensity level of three miles per hour, a duration of 45 minutes, and a frequency of four times a week.

It is also possible to organize yawing into categories. One form uses a hand to cover the open mouth, the intensity is a fully opened mouth, the duration is three seconds, and the frequency is once every five minutes. These behaviors are overt because they are observable to anyone who cares to pay attention.

Overt behavior is contrasted to covert behavior. These actions are not observable because they occur inside people's heads. They include thinking, daydreaming, wishing, and hoping. Often no one knows covert behaviors are happening except the person performing them.

COPING WITH AGGRESSIVE BEHAVIORS FROM BOSS

Aggressive behavior in the workplace puts employees at risk, hinders productivity, and hurts the company's reputation. Even when aggression isn't blatant, it eventually erodes trust and morale and could lead to increasingly violent behavior.

There's a common but unfortunate perception that bosses should be aggressive.

The idea is that things just can't get done unless someone is clobbering someone else to do it. Aggressive people aren't easily discouraged, are tenacious, and are motivated to meet their goals— or so the thinking goes.

What's true is that aggressive bosses are lousy bosses. Aggressive bosses have little regard for others' rights and boundaries, aren't concerned about others' needs, and make decisions based on their agendas, not what's best for employees or the company.

If you work for an aggressive boss, you may be confused, frustrated, angry, and anxious. Aggressive bosses have that effect.

Establish a Connection

Sometimes the best way to deal with an abusive boss is to establish commonality. Find something you have in common that you can focus on to start to build a professional relationship. If your boss is egotistical, choose something that he or she is specifically interested in, and ask about projects. If low emotional intelligence is the problem, choose something you're interested in that will make your boss sees you as a human being, not just another line item on his quarterly budget. Go out of your way to have a chat at lunch or on breaks – or if you have weekly meetings, lead with a quick "how's the project XYZ moving along?" to demonstrate your interest.

Increase Dependence

Decreasing dependence on an abusive supervisor (avoidance) creates a safe distance for the subordinate. But this does not motivate the supervisor to reform. Increasing a supervisor's dependence on the subordinate works better to break the spiral of abuse. Only then does self-interest kick in and drive positive change. This happens naturally when a supervisor recognizes a subordinate as instrumental for goal and resource attainment.

Don't stoop to their level.

When your boss employs passive-aggressive behavior, no doubt, you've been tempted to return the favor. If your inquiry about their obvious cold shoulder has been met with, "No, nothing's wrong, I don't know what you mean," you've probably at least entertained the idea of being curt and emotionless right back. But that doesn't work. Similarly, if you feel your boss has taken undue credit for your work, don't take the bait by going around the office privately, letting others know it was you who deserves it. Chances are they already know. You get far more respect by being the bigger person.

There are several problems with lowering yourself to reciprocal passive aggression. First, it only reinforces your boss's behavior by legitimizing it. Once you stoop to their level, you've colluded by creating an unspoken contract for how you intend to manage conflict with them, and using a more direct, mature approach later becomes inordinately difficult. Second, you're likely to contradict your values by behaving in ways you don't respect. Don't presume your boss is aware of and even being intentional with their behavior. More often, passive-aggressiveness is an unconscious response to anxiety or a perceived threat. At their core, these bosses tend to be lonely, deeply insecure, and perpetually anxious. As best as you can, adopt a compassionate rather than angry posture toward them.

Respectfully call the question.
Directly confronting a passive-aggressive boss is rife with risk. You're directly challenging someone who has made clear they don't want to be direct and has disproportionate power over your life. I saw this go sideways once when a fed-up leader said to her boss, "Don't think for a minute I don't see what you're doing here. I know for a fact you didn't forget about the meeting because I saw you write it down. Your passive-aggressive isn't fooling any of us." Those in earshot of her confrontation gave her high-fives for putting her foot down. But a week later she was fired. There are effective ways to raise your concerns without triggering the behavior you're trying to eliminate. While it may feel imbalanced, going the extra mile to make the relationship feel safe for your boss can have long-term benefits. Those inclined to employ passive-aggressive behavior tend to do it less when they think greater degrees of trust with others, so try to be non-judgmental and matter of fact.

Avoid conflict
Passive-aggressive leaders dislike any kind of conflict, healthy or otherwise. Every disagreement is seen as a confrontation, and any overt shows of emotion, especially anger, cause them significant discomfort and embarrassment. Obsessed with being well-liked and 'nice,' they rarely display overt anger. Instead, if you have initiated discussions or debates (which they will interpret as arguments or personal challenges, both intensely disliked), you may well suffer covert consequences: being left out of discussions, being the recipient of dismissive responses or suffering 'well-meaning, constructive' criticism at every opportunity.

CHARACTERISTICS OF THE AGGRESSIVE BOSS

Dishonest communicators
You can never get to the bottom of what was said. Conversations with staff are indirect, not entirely honest, and often ambiguous. Although passive-aggressive leaders are happy to talk for hours if given a chance, much of what is said is unnecessary or forgotten by the time the next meeting comes around. Listening is the breath they take between sentences. Lacking in focus, they are ill-equipped to think strategically or systematically.

Inconsistent
These leaders say one thing and do the exact opposite. They cannot tolerate being kept waiting but will invariably keep you waiting, procrastinating, and dawdling and always with an excellent excuse that keeps on coming.
The only pattern is, there is no pattern. Minds are changed frequently, and in the search for approval, they cannot take a decisive stand on any issue.

Undermine
Passive-aggressive leaders envy those who possess qualities they know they don't have or those who achieve high levels of success. Their way of dealing with feelings of inadequacy is to undermine the success of others. They will choose a skill or competency that a peer or direct report may not yet have mastered (but they have...) and make regular offhand comments (sarcastic and/or spiteful). If challenged, the fall-back position is always, "I'm only joking, where's your sense of humor?"
They cannot be honestly enthusiastic about the successes of others and do not like competition, especially from the employ-

ees. Always take care when using this person as a referee.

Lack Controlling
Power, control, and prestige are everything to the passive-aggressive leader, but they will NEVER admit to it. They are obsessed with control but do all they can to appear 'laid-back.' Ambitions are played down as the landscape is surveyed for opportunities for greater prestige.

They have a strong desire to be right and expect compliance. You'll never quite know where you stand: the indirect aggression, dishonesty, and the crippling need for control all create enormous difficulties in the workplace.

Low Emotional Intelligence
It's not surprising that passive-aggressive leaders lack self-esteem and have low levels of self-confidence. It's all an act. Overt confidence without an ounce of humility is a guaranteed indicator of deep-seated feelings of fear, of unworthiness. Poor self-awareness, coupled with a broken social antenna creates interactions that are disingenuous and lacking tact and insight. When it comes to daily dealings with employees, exchanges are all too often disrespectful, again with that irritatingly jovial overtone.

Passive-aggressive leaders cannot genuinely apologize for their behavior. Due to their inadequate levels of emotional intelligence, they lack the insight necessary to understand their behavior is inappropriate.

If your organization offers few avenues for self-expression and has an underpinning culture that discourages conflict, or challenges to the status quo, you may well be a breeding ground for passive-aggressive behavior. When people lack the authority or means to speak up, the resistance will emerge, indirectly and covertly.

Don't care about the truth.
Truth and fact are "bendable" according to the aggressive personality's desires. One day your boss gives X instruction for doing Y,

but when you do X, and the result (through no fault of yours) is unsatisfactory, the boss denies giving that instruction.

Don't know when to back off.
Ironically, aggressive employers will own this trait as a virtue and brag about their tenacity. However, this lack of "internal brakes," is not a positive quality. In extreme cases, this trait can lead to ethical and legal breaches.

It can be very childish.
At times, dealing with an aggressive boss feels like dealing with a child, and that's because aggressive bosses often exhibit child-like qualities. In the pursuit of their desires, they're immune to reason, logic, and common sense—just like a willful six-year-old.

COPING WITH AGGRESSIVE
BEHAVIORS FROM CO-WORKERS

Workplace aggression comes in several forms, with some more obvious than others. While many people picture overtly violent behaviors such as provoking a physical altercation, aggression can also manifest in more subtle but equally destructive actions. Some employees act out in passive-aggressive ways, such as consistently missing deadlines, showing up late for important meetings, or turning in subpar work. Other employees would never lay a hand on a colleague, but use verbal abuse to demean and intimidate. For example, they might call another employee an embarrassing nickname or belittle his work in front of others. If not addressed promptly, aggression can spiral into violence.

Understand Their Motivation
Though passive-aggressive behavior can be incredibly frustrating, it's a good idea to pause before you react to consider why your coworker might be acting this way.

It's helpful to separate the passive from the aggressive; The aggressive part is motivated by the same things that make anyone aggressive. Maybe your coworker feels wronged, threatened, or offended.

The more exciting part is what makes people passive, "I believe it is fear. Unfortunately, conflict between people has been dangerous or deadly throughout human history. It's natural — and even useful — to be conflict-averse. In passive-aggressive people, their fear stops them from being direct, but their aggression leads to them acting out or speaking up in passive ways."

While a direct conversation is certainly more efficient, when put in perspective, it's easy to understand why your colleague might take this approach. Knowing this can help you cool down any annoyance you're feeling as a result of their behavior for a more measured, logical response.

Don't Overreact or Lash Out

One of the biggest challenges of dealing with passive-aggressive people is controlling your own emotions, which, if allowed to get out of control, could harm your focus and performance.

"The biggest mistake we can make is letting passive-aggressive behaviors and personalities get to us, shake us and make us show up as less than who we aim to be every day," "We have to model the behavior we want to see in the workplace, so it's very important to not stoop below our values and behaviors of professionalism and strong communication."

The trick for managing difficult personalities at work? Imagine a snowglobe: "Inside the snowglobe is the situation you're dealing with, but outside of it is where you find yourself. This allows you to look at the situation objectively and helps you manage your own emotions and proceed more mindfully."

This exercise encourages you to remove yourself from the conflict and see it for what it is. "There's something powerful about objectivity in these very charged, uncomfortable situations with very frustrating people."

Be Honest

By not saying anything to your passive-aggressive colleague, you're essentially condoning their behavior.

"Find an appropriate and healthy way to surface the conflict using a lens of radical candor being honest while being kind," "This could look a variety of ways depending on the nature of the issue, severity and the players, however, the most important thing is not to sweep the issue under the rug."

Whether it's an informal conversation with them or a meeting with a mediator like someone from HR or a shared supervisor, finding a way to bring up their actions and let them know why you're speaking with them is an essential step.

Use Your Emotional Intelligence to Your Advantage

We hear a lot about the importance of empathy in the workplace, and this situation is a prime example of where it can be a huge advantage.

Understand that passive-aggressive people are doing the best they can. "It would be great if they could be more direct, but they are addressing issues the best way they know-how. By bringing strong emotional intelligence to conversations with them, you can help them feel safe so they can be more direct, and you can have a constructive conversation."

During your conversation with them, remember: "It doesn't matter who's right or who's doing it right," Crabtree says. "It's better to be effective than right. Helping people process their emotions, get clear on their needs, and responding to them appropriately can help [the] organization move forward."

The best way to accomplish this is by asking the right questions. "It's ten times more effective when you can try to put yourself in the passive-aggressive individual's shoes and try to understand where they are coming from."

That means asking probing questions and using phrases like: "Help me understand…" "I'm listening…" and "Can you fill me in…" The logic behind this? "All they want is to be heard." "If they are not sharing their frustration, verbally communicate to them that they can trust you and share their true thoughts and feelings. This enables them to feel more comfortable and share more openly."

Build a Relationship

Once you've solved your initial conflict with your passive-aggressive coworker, you'll want to build a foundation for avoiding future issues with them. "I would try to focus on building a relationship with them." Once they trust you, their guard will go down, and they will use less passive-aggression.

Ideally, once they realize you're not a threat, they'll feel more comfortable coming straight to you with issues.

Look at the Bigger Picture

If you spot this behavior in multiple colleagues, consider that the issue might have more to do with corporate culture than the individual. Passive-aggressive behavior may indicate low workplace morale if many people are using this tactic. These employees do not feel connected to the company. They may not trust they can share their true feelings. Create an open, honest, trusting workplace, and everyone will thrive.

Find your allies

The reality of dealing with an aggressive colleague is that you're probably not the only person facing their behavior, and there's no point in suffering alone. Your first point of contact should be your colleagues, ask them how they manage this behavior, and use them as support when necessary.

Just make sure it comes across as asking for advice and not moaning, mainly if the person you're having trouble with is another woman.

Put yourself in their shoes

We're all creatures of habit, and so most people's behavior can be worked out fairly quickly. First, identify the type of person you're dealing with; are they an optimist or pessimist, do they like making quick decisions or take time to think things over, do they focus on the big picture or want to know all the details? Once you know this, you can reflect that back at them. For example, when pitching your big idea to a pessimist, make sure you point out the potential problems, and explain how you would address them before they have a chance to.

Bring it back to you

Most aggressive people like to dominate the conversation, so it helps to remind them that they're dealing with a real person and that their behavior has an effect on you. Bringing the conversation back to how you're feeling and what you're thinking can be a way to move beyond their demands. Using "I" sentences, such as "I find it helpful when you..." or "I would like to talk about...", to remind them there's another person in the conversation.

Stand up for yourself (or find someone who will)

If you're in a negotiation or difficult meeting with someone who doesn't want to let you speak, then it's essential to make sure that your words have power. Whitmell suggests asking your boss for assertiveness training to make sure you're confident standing your ground and can express yourself firmly. If you're dealing with an office bully, now one quick tip is to make sure that your boss or another colleague is in meetings with you or copied on emails between the two of you. It's much easier for your colleagues to think that aggressive behavior is ok when there's no-one else watching.

Push back

Aggression is often just tactical behavior, and so a simple way to deal with it is by calling the other person out. If you know them well, he suggests, go with a light tone and something like "just imagine how much better this conversation would go if neither of us attacked the other?" or a more formal "I feel like there's quite a hostile atmosphere in the room right now, how do you feel?". Bringing their behavior out into the open will force them to address it, and you'll feel like you've regained some control over the situation. And if they're really difficult, then sit back quietly and let them bluster themselves out.

EXAMPLES OF APPROVAL-SEEKING BEHAVIORS

Taking disagreement personally.
When someone disagrees with something you've said or done, do you take it to heart as a personal slight and feel upset or even insulted?
This is a typical response for a people pleaser because the quest for approval has failed.

Changing or adapting your point of view in the face of apparent disapproval.
You've voiced your opinion on some matter, essential or not, and someone responds with an opposing view.
Do you vigorously defend your position or find yourself softening your argument to fit more closely with theirs?
An approval seeker's opinion changes depending on who they're talking to because they lack confidence in their convictions and are keen not to alienate others by adopting a conflicting view.

Afraid to say 'no' for fear of disapproval.
Are you a serial over-committer? Do you always say 'yes' when asked to do something when your instinctive response is to say 'no'?
Physical and emotional exhaustion is the result of this behavior and leads you to resent all the things you've committed to.
But it stems from the need to please and your quest for approval.

Not standing up for your rights.
Being a human doormat – to be walked over by whoever chooses to do so – is so much easier than saying, "Hey, no, that's not fair" and standing up for yourself.

Failing to draw a line and say 'no' reinforces your lack of self-belief and even causes others to think less of you.

Gaining attention or acceptance through gossip.
Do you feel the urge to tell tales to make yourself look better or smarter or more knowledgeable?

Sharing gossip gives you the power to impress others, to be the center of attention, and to gain kudos. This temporarily bolsters your low self-esteem.

Appearing to agree with someone (verbally/non-verbally) when you don't.
How often do you find yourself listening to an enthusiastically expressed opinion that you don't agree with, but appear to agree with nonetheless?

By expressing support for a view you don't agree with, either with words or a nod of your head, you're not being true to yourself. You want that person to approve of you and like you.

Not complaining when you've received unsatisfactory service or goods.
How many times have you moaned and groaned about the food or the service in a restaurant, but when the waiter cheerfully asks if everything's okay, nodded your head and said everything's fine and dandy?

The worst you might do is to leave a smaller tip.

Or you bought something which isn't fit for purpose, but you don't dare to return it to the store.

By not taking issue with these things, you're reinforcing your lack of self-worth. You're telling yourself you are not entitled to the best of anything.

Pretending to know or understand something.
That awkward moment when someone assumes that you know something or have a particular skill...

...the approval seeker's default response in such a situation is to fake it.

The thing is, nine times out of ten, the pretense is exposed.

Sadly, as you'll probably have discovered, rather than gaining the approval you seek, you get condemnation or ridicule instead.

Feeling the need to apologize even when there's been no disapproval.

No matter what has happened and whether or not you had any hand in it – and even if no word of blame has been voiced – the people-pleaser will always be the first to apologize.

If there is no error or behavioral faux pas on your part, why should you feel the need to apologize?

Expecting compliments or fishing for them and being upset, they're not forthcoming.

Few things provide the validation you desire better than a compliment.

An approval seeker may set out deliberately, however, to coerce those they're interacting with into voicing praise.

Often, that praise is neither due nor appropriate.

An extension of this type of behavior is to feel upset when the compliments you desire fail to materialize.

Failing to cope with any level of criticism.

If you aim to gain the approval of others, then the concept of criticism is utterly intolerable. It implies you have failed in some way in achieving your goal.

This response is often rooted in childhood when parental criticism or even punishment for failed goals or tasks drove us on to seek approval next time.

Behaving in a way that's contrary to your own beliefs.

This is typical behavior in high school: joining the gang to be among the 'popular' people, even if, in your heart of hearts, you disagree with what they say and do.

That's forgivable as a teenager, but not so much when you're an adult.

An approval seeker can easily find themselves in a situation where they don't follow their heart. They follow their people-pleasing head instead, even if this creates a conflict with their core beliefs.

OVERCOMING APPROVAL BEHAVIORS

Whether you're trying to get hundreds of likes on social media platforms or hoping to connect with someone on popular mobile applications, sometimes it can seem like our happiness depends on other people in today's society. But there are ways to stop seeking approval of others. The key is to begin with addressing your thought process. Rather than seeking support from external influences, try to find true happiness by developing a more stable relationship within yourself.

"It's exhausting trying to be everything to everyone. But more to the point, it's unsustainable. Eventually, the psyche just collapses in on itself, like a sinkhole of muck, pressured by the weight of trying to figure out who other people want you to be. To be truly happy, you must honor the truth of you. But all too often, finding this truth is profoundly complicated.

Feeling confident without anyone else's approval means loving yourself first and knowing your self-worth. "You can't give away something you don't own already. You have to love yourself first."

Become Aware Of Your Actions
"The first step to stop seeking approval of others is to become aware [that] we are stuck on doubt, insecurity, or uncertainty. We must recognize that our actions (of seeking approval) come from the emotions and beliefs that arise within us," Once you become aware of how often you're seeking approval from others, you can begin to work on yourself from within.

Develop A Greater Sense Of Self-Worth
Sometimes you can be your own worst enemy by having negative thoughts about yourself. But quashing these is key to recognizing

your worth.

"Self-worth is knowing you are loved, valuable, and worthy simply because you are, and not because of what you think, say, do, or what others think of you. We tend to seek approval from others when our sense of self-worth is low when we believe we have to 'perform' to be worthy of attention and love.

Learn To Accept Yourself For Who You Are

Don't worry about what other people are thinking, but instead solely focus on what makes you happy. "It can be challenging to accept all parts of ourselves, but that is genuinely where self-confidence begins. As we accept who we are, we find we don't need others' approval or input anymore, because we know the truth about ourselves.

Make Friends With Rejection

Think back to a time when you failed to meet expectations or disappointed someone. Maybe your boss asked you to completely re-do a project, or perhaps you forgot an important deadline. How did you recover from that slip-up? What did you learn as a result? In most cases, you were probably able to turn the situation around—and it likely helped you grow as a professional.

When you break it down, disapproval is a form of feedback—information you can use to improve and make your next performance even stronger. It also helps to reframe rejection as something positive. It means you're moving forward and pushing limits, rather than just staying in your comfort zone.

Embrace a Growth Mindset

When you prioritize learning and constant improvement, you free yourself from needing approval from others. Individuals who viewed skill and ability as something to be developed over time, rather than innate and unchangeable, were most likely to achieve their full potential. Those with this "growth mindset" were more likely to challenge themselves than those with "fixed mindsets," who took feedback as a sign of disapproval and failure.

By understanding that there is abundant room for growth, improvement, and success, you can wean yourself from the constant need for validation.

Focus on the Process, Not Outcomes

If you're prone to approval-seeking, focus on improving processes, rather than achieving a particular outcome. When you focus too narrowly on one single result, such as getting a promotion or raise, you attach your self-worth to external standards—which may be outside of your control.

For example, even if you're performing well and hitting all your benchmarks, your company might not be doing as well and decide to put a salary freeze into effect. While this is entirely outside of your control and doesn't reflect on your value as an employee, if you've been banking on that raise, you're bound to be disappointed.

However, if you instead concentrate on a process that you can control, you can reduce the power that approval has over you. For example, maybe you strive to become more organized, so you've seen as more effective—and therefore, more deserving of a promotion.

The only person you need to answer to is yourself. Your self-approval is a crucial aspect of your integrity and will keep you happy and fulfilled in the long run. By working to free yourself from approval-seeking behaviors at work, you're honoring yourself and your needs—and setting yourself up for long-term happiness.

Check The Accuracy Of Your Beliefs

While there's nothing wrong with collaborating with other people, you don't want to be persuaded because you may not truly believe in your voice yet. "By checking the accuracy of your beliefs, you will recognize that your story is not stable and therefore will be able to consider other perspectives, such as: 'I can consider I am good enough,' or 'I can consider I am equal to everyone else,' or 'I can consider the only person who can genuinely grant me confidence in myself.

Practice Self-Love

Remember to be just as kind to yourself as you are to your friends. "This includes doing kind things for yourself, practicing self-care, and letting others love you, as well as practicing self-compassion. As we build our self-worth, our need to seek approval will diminish dramatically.

Try To Understand Why You're Seeking Approval

Comprehending why you're always seeking approval from others can make it easier to eliminate the behavior. "Before you turn to others for support, stop and ask yourself, 'What do I think about this?' Then, 'Why don't I trust my own opinion in this matter?. Perhaps you'll find you are seeking approval because you're uncertain, or maybe you feel certain, but you're seeking support because you want someone else to like or accept you. Understanding the motive behind your need for support is an essential step in overcoming it.

Journal Your Thoughts

While writing is already considered to be therapeutic, it can help you figure out your internal struggles, too. "Each day, write a full page in a journal of just your top of head thoughts. At the end of the week, go through the journal and circle consistent thoughts and feelings. Then on Friday, make a list of the transcendent idea you had throughout the week and the circled words in your journal.

Ask Where Your Need for Approval Comes From

In many cases, a tendency to seek approval at work stems from something in your past. For example, were you taught to respect authority growing up? If so, you may feel uncomfortable expressing disagreement in work contexts. Did you struggle to make friends in school and develop a fear of being rejected? This may now be driving you to do whatever it takes to feel included and liked by your co-workers.

Reflect on how your childhood or early development may be contributing to your current approval-seeking behavior.

Trust Yourself

Don't let anyone else tell you your choices are not good enough. "Hold on to your truth and allow it to absorb into your psyche. When you find yourself going into judgment around it, label the judgment as defeating thoughts and push them away.

Try To Think Like A Millennial

"The Millennial Generation is less likely to do this because they're generally more comfortable with themselves. "It's probably because of how they were brought up by everyone 'being awarded' for just participating. It's a belief that they have enough confidence with what they choose to bring to the table." While this might sound silly, mostly, you just want to gain enough confidence in yourself, so you can automatically believe in the decisions you make.

Stop Comparing Yourself To Others

Just because you're not going down the same path as other people doesn't mean it's the wrong path. Realize you are a unique being with a singular purpose and path in this world, any comparison or need for another's approval is apples to oranges. And, if you are tempted to compare to motivate you to be a better self, just remember to take those comparisons with a grain of salt; you might be comparing your real body to a photo-shopped one, your organic life to a fabricated depiction, or your role models might be reality TV stars who get paid to memorize and read scripts.

Continue To Practice

Practice makes perfect, right? Remember that this new thought process is not going to change overnight. Don't expect yourself to change overnight. Be kind and gentle with yourself in this process. In no time at all, you will begin to experience a sense of well-being. This sense of well-being will grow into a generalized feeling of happiness, that you are safe and secure, content with who you are rather than who you think others want you to be.

Take A Break From Social Media

Sometimes you just need to take a break from being overstimulated by social media. Try to focus on other things (like fixing up your resume or reading a new book) to help your mind unwind. In a world full of media — social, television, print, and beyond — we're bombarded with images of idealism. We end up in a state of constant social comparison to others, knowing someone else had '100 likes/claps' and needing the same to feel validated. We become addicted to seeking approval through "likes/claps" and other external accolades. We end up diminishing, second-guessing, and getting down on ourselves for all of the things we haven't yet accomplished or acquired if we don't get that approval.

Become Attuned With Your Inner Voice

Learning to trust your gut can be one of the best things you can do for yourself. It can help you understand the path you're supposed to take, and feel more confident in the direction you're going. "If we practice, we can become so attuned to our inner voice that we always know what it's telling us and where it's guiding us, which is in the right direction. We only get steered wrong when we stop paying attention to our inner voice and start paying attention to outside ones. The only approval we need is from ourselves, and that keeps control squarely within us.

For you to truly love who you are as a person, you should stop worrying about what everyone else is thinking. Be proud of yourself, and hopefully, you will stop seeking the approval of others after using reading this book.

AVOID BEING UNDERMINED

Undermine means to make someone less confident, less power-ful, or less likely to succeed, or to make something weaker, often gradually. Here are ways to avoid being undermined:

Report It Once It Affects Your Work

Once this undermining starts impeding your output, you should take concrete steps to alter the situation.

First off, confront the people talking about you. If you know who they are, have a simple talk with each person one-on-one, and explain that you want the behavior to stop. This is often the most effective way to solve the problem.

But if your plea falls on deaf ears, take it up the chain of command. Talk to your manager, your department head, Human Resources, and so on. File a formal complaint with HR stating just the facts. Make it clear you will not accept this behavior.

Pack Your Bags

The simplest option is to weigh your pros and cons and figure out whether it's worth the mental aggravation to come in every day and work in a pit of vipers.

If your "cons" column weighs heavier, then begin a new job search and find a friendlier workplace.

TIP: Read the reviews of your next company at websites. Those anonymous reviews typically spill all the beans.

Just remember: no company is perfect.

Control What You Can: Yourself

Finally, the age-old adage is true: you can only control your re-action to a situation. You can't control what other people say about you or your work.

If they're catty or passive-aggressive, you can choose to ignore them and refuse to take the bait. If they're hostile, you can choose to walk away.

Meanwhile, you continue to do the work you were hired for to the best of your ability. Because doing it any other way (i.e., slacking off and choosing to produce mediocre work) is an insult both to your capabilities as a performer and to your employer's trust in you.

You Can Only Do So Much

Excellence is divisive in an organization where mediocrity rules. But realize that you can only do so much to fit in or to try and change the culture before you are tainted. Better to find a company where your skills and your drive can be appreciated. And where, instead of worrying about colleagues stabbing you in the back, you work with people who have your back.

Check with others

Check with other coworkers to see if the undermining is happening to them too. If it's undermining, the chances are that it is. Keep in mind that the purpose of these conversations is information gathering, not gossiping, and not bashing the undermining coworker. Engaging in the latter behaviors will only make the situation more complicated and worse.

If you find out others are being sabotaged as well, you can either handle the situation as a group or keep them in mind when you handle the situation yourself.

Document your concerns

Save emails and other correspondence with the underminer. Keep notes on undercutting behaviors with dates and times of occurrences.

Keep everything transparent

Copy others on emails involving the underminer or undermining behaviors, including your boss, when it makes sense to do so. This is key when dealing with an underminer because they thrive by engaging in sneaky activities. If you bring everything out into the open, you severely hamper the underminer's efforts.

Maintain relationships with boss and colleagues

Continue to build your relationship with your boss. One way to do so is with regular meetings if your boss is willing to do that. The more your boss knows you care about your work, and the better your boss knows you, the less a coworker will be able to undermine you successfully.

The same is true of your colleagues. The better the work you do for them, the less likely your coworker will be able to undermine you to them effectively. The more champions you have, the less someone can truly sabotage you, no matter how hard he tries. Building relationships with your colleagues is key to your career advancement for a wide variety of reasons.

Specific to dealing with subversion, if the underminer is hiding things from you, your network of colleagues will be invaluable. Make sure you're getting useful information from your network or other sources, so you don't look inept, unprepared, or out of touch.

Take a direct approach

When the undermining coworker does something concrete, approach him about it. For example, if a coworker leaves you out of a meeting, ask him why. If he continues to do it and you go to your boss about it, your attempt to resolve the problem directly with the offender and your documentation of the issue should go a long way with your boss.

If a promotion is up for grabs, make clear to your boss that you want it. Sometimes we assume that our boss knows we want a promotion, but always be direct in telling your boss that you wish to the position and are ready for it.

Remain professional

Throughout all of this, keep things in perspective and be calm, concise, and prepared. Stick to the facts of the situation. For example, you might say, "My challenge is that Joe no longer includes me in the monthly meetings we have with IT for a project we're working on." Contrast that with inserting personal, emotional, or opinion into what you report to your boss.

For example, avoid saying something like, "Joe is so selfish. All he cares about is himself and whether or not he looks good to IT!" Not only will this take away from your credibility, but it also doesn't give your boss anything concrete to work with. Even if you're right and Joe is selfish, your boss can't fix that.

Your boss can only try to correct behaviors, which is why you solely want to present facts. Always remember that while you can handle your personal life any way that you want to, this is your workplace. It would help if you remained professional and fact-based.

For mental health purposes, do remember that this is only the work portion of your life, and this, too, shall pass. It's just something you have to get through and deal with. Rise above the drama, and do not let the undercutting decrease your confidence. I have watched great employees start to question themselves because of undermining coworkers or even undermining bosses. Don't let that happen to you. Keep your head held high and try to combat the sabotage with the information in this article.

If all else fails, consider moving on

If it seems like your boss and your organization will not support you in your efforts to address the undermining, it's probably time to move on. Do your best at your current job, search for a new role, and leave as soon as you find the right opportunity.

You may wonder why an organization wouldn't address undermining if you present them with facts, but some workplaces are toxic or aren't a good fit for you. It's okay to acknowledge that, keep the relationships you have with your champions, and move on to a new employer.

SIGNS OF UNDERMINING COWORKERS

They're competitive in an unproductive way

Competition can be healthy, so not everyone you compete with is undercutting you. Those who undermine engage in an unhealthy form of competition.

For example, they may act like they've worked at your company longer than you even if they haven't, saying something like, "We've done it that way for the last five years," when you've been there six years, and your underminer has been there three years.

Another example of this unhealthy competition is someone shooting down everything you suggest or do, often in front of others, or correcting you in front of colleagues, the legal team, and your boss.

Competitiveness and outright sabotage are often difficult to tell apart, but the latter is comparatively rare.

Before you label someone as an underminer, make sure they're not just hypercompetitive. If your coworker is overly competitive, then they will want to beat out everyone. If they are actively undermining you, then they want to see *you* fail in particular.

The two aren't mutually exclusive, but it's still an important distinction.

They put you on the defensive

You never argue with this particular colleague, but he or she always manages to put you on the defensive.

If someone's making you feel like you're on trial, then that's not a good sign. They might be baiting you and waiting for you to slip up.

They put negative thoughts in your head

Someone who is actively undermining you is likely to put nega-tive thoughts in your head or tell you negative stories to get you ginned up and make you unhappy with your boss, your col-leagues, your work, or the workplace.

For example, he might say something like, "Why do you and I do all of the work for legal?" or "Senior management needs to pro-vide us with more resources like automated workflows!"

The underminer's goal is to make you disgruntled because you'll be less likely to form connections with others and less effect-ive in your role. This allows the underminer to more effectively make you look bad to your colleagues and causes you to under-perform in your role.

They take credit or place blame

An underminer is likely to take credit for your work or take full credit for something you worked on together. For example, if you draft a template agreement with your underminer, he is likely to tell your colleagues that he drafted an agreement for their use without ever mentioning your contributions.

On the flip side, someone who undermines may also blame you for her shortcomings. For example, if a sales representative you work with provides the wrong version of an agreement to a cli-ent, she may blame you, telling you that she gave the client the version you provided to her even if that's not true.

They gossip — a lot

Everyone partakes in a bit of workplace gossip every once in a while. Sometimes, it's the only way to figure out what's going on at your job.

Still, it's not a good sign if one of your colleagues seems to con-tinually have his or her finger on the pulse of every nasty tale cir-culating the office.

If your coworker is a gossip-monger, then who's to say that they aren't talking about you behind your back?

Someone who is trying to undermine you will likely badmouth others to you and you to others. Underminers criticize but offer no solutions because their goal is to make people look bad, not improve anything. Underminers think they look better if they make others look worse.

They try to distract you

If your colleague is continuously distracting you from your job, then they might be an innocuous and slightly lonely procrastinator.

But if you feel like someone is intentionally attempting to derail your productivity, then that's a problem.

They withhold necessary information from you

Someone who is sabotaging you may withhold essential information from you to thwart your work. Perhaps an underminer will give you an incorrect date, thus, making you miss a deadline or not give you all the relevant information so that, unbeknownst to you, you don't do your best work.

They act like your supervisor

If the person subverting you is your lateral or is titled down the chain of command from you, he may start treating you like a direct report. For example, he may assign you to work or talk to you like he's senior to you. This may take place in front of others. The underminer's goal is to make you feel less than him and, if done in front of others, to establish himself as the go-to resource among your colleagues.

They direct sabotaging comments and behavior at others as well

This is an exciting hallmark of underminers. Usually, sandbagging behavior is not targeted. It's often directed at multiple people. For example, you may have an attorney colleague who you think is undercutting you, and you may observe him sabotaging others. For instance, if the legal assistant ("Jane") takes a day off, the underminer might loudly say to the boss, "Where is Jane today?!"

When the boss responds that she took the day off, the underminer may reply, loudly, "Oh, okay, I'll just mail this myself." If it's part of an overall pattern, this is classic undermining behavior. It's subtle, but it points out to the boss that the assistant is not available for him when he needs her. Even if she has a legitimate day off, the underminer's goal is to put negative thoughts about the assistant in the boss' head.

They interfere with your productivity

To weaken your reputation, underminers may try to interfere with your productivity. Perhaps your underminer will stop by your office for an extended visit to keep you from doing your work. Or maybe she will encourage you to take a long lunch.

This is the tricky part of being undercut; some of the underminer's behavior seems friendly. You may think, "How nice to suggest I unwind with a long lunch!" If a well-intentioned co-worker suggested this, it would be thoughtful, but not when your underminer suggests it. Your underminer has nefarious motives.

They're fake

Underminer's words often don't match their behavior. You may think that you imagine the subversive behavior because the person doing it may be very friendly to your face, even acting like your buddy. Many of an underminer's activities require some closeness or bond, so they are fake to have access to you to put negative thoughts in your head or to perform the other negative behaviors in this article.

They're envious of your success

An underminer is not happy when you succeed. If you get a promotion, the person torpedoing you is already finding ways to take that promotion from you or get herself promoted. Underminers think of work success as a zero-sum game. If you have more success, underminers feel like they are losing somehow.

Healthy coworkers can enjoy your achievements because they understand that multiple people can flourish in the workplace, but an underminer envies your good fortune and resents you for it. As much as it is essential to be positive in the workplace, the underminer will prey on your positivity and use it to sabotage you subtly. Thus, if you recognize that someone is undercutting you, keep in mind that she is not happy about your advancement, or her bad behavior may blindside you.

They socially ostracize you

Your underminer may leave you out of social outings with colleagues or make rude or nasty comments, or backhanded insults in front of others. This is all part of the underminer's effort to subtly isolate you to undermine you in front of your colleagues.

For example, an attorney senior to you may drop an offhand comment about how she would not take your job because it would be beneath her level. This minimizes your role to your colleagues without being hostile. It's subtle but effective.

They act like the victim

The exciting part about an underminer is that, although they're victimizing you, they often act like the victim. For example, someone who is undercutting you may socially ostracize you, then act like you're leaving him out when you bond with others at work.

They treat others a certain way

Interestingly, you can often identify an underminer by the way he treats others. For example, if you witness someone treating your colleagues in a way that minimizes their importance, you may be in the presence of an underminer.

If you see someone acting more demanding and entitled than cooperative and collaborative in the workplace, you may be in the presence of an underminer. If you observe someone only focusing on his achievements and not the triumphs of those around him, you may be in the presence of an underminer.

They influence others to treat you differently

If someone you always got along well with suddenly starts to give you the cold shoulder for seemingly no reason, this is one of the most concerning signs that you're being undermined because this means that the undermining is working, at least with the person who is acting differently towards you. It is imperative to take steps to guard against any additional undermining.

COVERT BEHAVIOURS

Covert behaviors are unobservable actions which can only be deduced by oneself. A huge majority of psychologists reason that behaviors are only eternal actions and behaviors which are observable. However, the behavior is psychophysical in origin, and both internal and external worlds play an equal role in the occurrence of the behavior. Anything that brings alteration in the environment can be categorized as behavior, which means even when the actions are unobservable, they are behaviors. Examples of these covert behaviors are; perceiving, remembering, reasoning, thinking, creating, and dreaming, among many more.

The main reason, unobservable actions are not considered as behaviors are because such behaviors are not deducible to audiences. But, covert behaviors are of huge influence on overt behaviors.
For instance, *thinking, reasoning, reading* in silence are covert behaviors, hidden behaviors, but these behaviors directly impact the way the person behaves in the actions they perform.

In the broader sense, even hidden behaviors bring alteration to the environment, and hence they must be classified as behaviors. Also, psychologists and behaviorists believe that covert behaviors are essential in the subject of psychology inquiry. These unseen actions are what influence any actions of the individual. Although the study of these covert behaviors isn't easy to conduct, documentation and joint research can lead to significant discoveries of individual behaviors, state of mind in different circumstances, analyzing the behaviors, and so on.

PASSIVE AGGRESSIVENESS

Passive-aggressive behavior is when one person is subtly aggressive towards another. This behavior aims to punish or retaliate to a perceived slight. A person exhibiting this behavior will use passive-aggressive actions rather than communicating their dissatisfaction with words. When you have been the target of this behavior, you may not realize that a person's hostility was purposeful. You may be left wondering why the person treated you poorly. Was it an accident? Are you too sensitive?

Passive-aggressive behavior is a pattern of indirectly expressing negative feelings instead of openly addressing them. There's a disconnect between what a passive-aggressive person says and what he or she does.

People with passive-aggressive behavior express their negative feelings subtly through their actions instead of handling them directly. This creates a separation between what they say and what they do.

Someone who uses passive aggression doesn't express negative feelings directly. Though they feel angry, resentful, or frustrated, they act neutral, pleasant, or even cheerful. They then find indirect ways to show how they feel.

Passive aggression isn't a mental illness. But people with mental health conditions may act that way. If you find yourself behaving like that, it could damage your personal and professional relationships.

For example, a passive-aggressive person might appear to agree perhaps even enthusiastically with another person's request. Rather than complying with the request, however, he or she might express anger or resentment by failing to follow through or missing deadlines.

Another example, say someone proposes a plan at work. A person with passive-aggressive behavior may oppose the plan, but instead of voicing their opinion, they say that they agree with it. Since they're actually against the plan, however, they resist following it. They may purposely miss deadlines, turn up late to meetings, and undermine the plan in other ways.

Here's another example: A woman is studying with her boyfriend in the same room. She is upset with him, but instead of telling him that she is mad at him, she blasts the music on their laptop to bother him.

In psychology, passive-aggressive behavior is characterized by a constant pattern of non-active resistance to expected work requirements, opposition, sullenness, stubbornness, and negative attitudes in response to requirements for normal performance levels expected by others. Most frequently, it occurs in the workplace, where resistance is exhibited by indirect behaviors as procrastination, forgetfulness, and purposeful inefficiency, especially in reaction to demands by authority figures. Still, it can also occur in interpersonal contexts.

Passive-aggressive behavior is also characterized as a personality trait marked by a pervasive pattern of negative attitudes and characterized by passive, sometimes obstructionist resistance to complying with expectations in interpersonal or occupational situations.

Passive-aggressive behavior from workers and managers is damaging to team unity and productivity. The worst case of passive-aggressive behavior involves destructive attitudes such as negativity, sullenness, resentment, procrastination, 'forgetting' to do something, chronic lateness, and intentional inefficiency. If this behavior is ignored, it could result in decreased office efficiency and frustration among workers. If managers are passive-aggressive in their behavior, it can end up stifling team creativity. It would make perfect sense that those promoted to leadership positions might often be those who on the surface appear to be agreeable, diplomatic and supportive, yet who are dishonest, backstabbing saboteurs behind the scenes.

Signs of passive-aggressive behavior:

- bitterness and hostility toward other peoples' requests
- intentionally delaying or making mistakes when dealing with other peoples' requests
- having a cynical, pessimistic, or aggressive demeanor
- frequently complaining about feeling underappreciated or deceived

Passive-aggressive behavior can be a symptom of several mental disorders, but it's not considered to be a distinct mental health condition. This type of behavior can affect a person's ability to create and maintain healthy relationships and can cause problems at work. However, there are ways to manage passive-aggressive behavior so that it doesn't have a negative impact on someone's quality of life.

There is usually some disconnect between what a person with passive-aggressive behavior says and what they do. Their behavior often angers family members, friends, and co-workers. However, the person may not be aware of their passive-aggressive behavior.

Signs of this type of behavior include:
- frequently criticizing or protesting
- being disagreeable or irritable
- procrastinating or being forgetful
- performing tasks inefficiently
- acting hostile or cynical
- acting stubborn
- blaming others
- complaining about being unappreciated
- displaying resentment over the demands of others

Causes of Passive-aggressive behavior

Passive-aggressive behaviors can have grave consequences on relationships between people in families, romances, and even in the workplace. So why is this often destructive behavior so common? The exact cause of passive-aggressive behavior isn't known. However, both biological and environmental factors may contribute to the development of passive-aggressive behavior.

Researchers believe people who exhibit passive-aggressive behaviors begin doing so in childhood. Parenting style, family dynamics, and other childhood influences may be contributing factors. Child abuse, neglect, and harsh punishment can also cause a person to develop passive-aggressive behaviors. Substance abuse and low self-esteem are even thought to lead to this type of behavior.

Underlying health conditions may result in behaviors that appear similar to passive-aggressive behavior. Some conditions associated with passive-aggressive behavior include:

- attention deficit hyperactivity disorder (ADHD)
- stress
- anxiety disorders
- depression
- conduct disorder
- oppositional defiant disorder
- bipolar disorder
- schizotypal personality disorder
- schizophrenia
- alcohol abuse

Upbringing: Some suggest that passive-aggressive behavior may stem from being raised in an environment where the direct expression of emotions was discouraged or not allowed. People may feel that they cannot express their real feelings more openly, so they may instead find ways to channel their anger or frustration passively.

- **Situational characteristics:** The situation also in-fluences passive-aggressive behavior. When you are in a situation where displays of aggression are not socially acceptable, such as at a business or family function, you might be more inclined to respond in a covert way when someone makes you angry.
- **Taking the easy road:** Being assertive and emotionally open is not always easy. When standing up for yourself is difficult or even scary, passive-aggression might seem like a more natural way to deal with your emotions without having to confront the source of your anger.

RECOGNIZING PASSIVE AGGRESSIVE BEHAVIOR

These telltale signs can usually recognize a person who engages in passive-aggressive behaviors:

Sullen, insulting, or negative communication

A person may be combative in their communication with you, taking everything you say negatively. They may constantly complain about things they see as wrong, act in a consistently grumpy manner, or be sullen in most of their communication with others — especially if it's about something they are responsible for or goal-directed. When they come, insults are not direct — they are subtle and could be taken either way (but are always meant in the negative).

They go silent, obstruct, or withhold

A passive-aggressive person may also go silent and withhold communication or information from you as a form of manipulation. They may refuse to talk about a topic, or end a discussion with, "You always get your way." If you need information, intimacy, communication, or some other kind of support, they withhold it as a form of punishment. If you need a specific piece of information or help from them, they may keep it from you. If they know they can hinder your goals or progress, they will find fault with every choice you offer them.

They regularly deny, forget, or procrastinate

Rather than acknowledge a failure to perform or to do something agreed-upon, they will fall back on excuses such as, "I forgot." They may deny that you both agreed on a course of action or some goal they were going to finish. Or they put off things regularly and consistently because they don't like rigid schedules or goal-setting imposed on them. They may not follow through on their responsibilities or duties, and then pull out, "I forgot" or "I just didn't have time to do that yet" as a catch-all excuse. Or deny you ever even discussed the matter.

Noncommittal in their agreement

People who are passive-aggressive are nearly always noncommittal in their agreement with something they disagree with. They are masters of ambiguity, ensuring that you never quite know where they stand on the issue. They avoid being pinned down to anything they don't agree with—but never express that disagreement directly.

Doing it half-assed

When the person doesn't want to do something, they'll do it in a way that ensures it will have to be redone. Or that it will take much longer than planned. Or it'll be done, but with no attention to detail or care about the result of the final product. They will, of course, deny any knowledge about the quality of their work, blame others, and play the victim.

Struggle between independence and dependence

People who are passive-aggressive struggle with expressing their independence in a socially-acceptable way. Instead, they do so in a stubborn, obstructionist manner, in a frustrating attempt to exert some control over their life. They are often unassertive and don't know how to be more decisive and sure of themselves, or how to express such assertiveness positively.

HOW TO DEAL WITH PASSIVE AGGRESSIVE BEHAVIOR

After you've determined you're likely dealing with someone who is engaging in multiple instances of passive-aggressive behavior, what can you do?

Do not react to their behavior
They are looking for a reaction from you to confirm their behavior has had its intended impact. If you get angry at them, you're just going to make the situation worse. "You're just passive-aggressive" won't help either. Any adverse reaction by you is going to reinforce them — and encourage them to continue acting in the same manner. This is the hardest part of dealing with a passive-aggressive person.

Do not blame or judge
It's easy to cast blame and judgment on a person when they seem to be looking for someone to join them in those kinds of behaviors. Don't make it about the person, and don't say things such as, "Well, you agreed to this deadline; why isn't it done?" That draws you into their world of negativity, obstruction, and denial. If they aren't put in a position to be on the defensive, they'll be more open to your suggestions.

Engage positively and assertively
Instead, it helps to engage positively and assertively with the person, focusing on the specific goals or issues under discussion. "How can we help move forward together on this project" or "What can we do to reach a decision that will work for both of us?" Be inclusive and ensure the person feels like they are a valued, important part of the decision or effort.

Be specific and invoke empathy

Be as specific as possible, and gently remind them about how the issue or problem is affecting you or the larger team or project. For instance, if the two of you are planning a vacation together but the person isn't helping make a final decision about your destination, you might try, "I'm so looking forward to spending this time alone with you. It means a lot to me to do this with you, so which of these two destinations works best for you?" At work, it might go something like, "While it's disappointing we couldn't get this done today, how much time do you need to complete it? Would Monday work for you? I know [fellow team member] Jill is looking forward to working with you on the next phase of the project."

Remove yourself

If nothing works or for your mental health benefits, you may not be able to deal with someone who is passive-aggressive regularly. In such instances, it's best to keep your interactions to a minimum, very goal-directed, and very specific. If they can't or won't perform at work, find another colleague to take this person's place. If you're in a relationship with this person, maybe it's a sign the relationship isn't offering nearly as many benefits as you thought.

If you feel that passive-aggressive behavior is damaging your relationships, there are steps you can take to change how you relate to others.

Improve your self-awareness

Passive-aggressive actions sometimes stem from not having a good understanding of why you are upset or what you are feeling. Start paying attention to what is going on as you react to different people and situations.

Give yourself time to make changes

Recognizing your behaviors is an excellent first step toward change, but altering your patterns and reactions can take some time.

Practice expressing yourself

Understanding your emotions and learning to express your feelings appropriately is an essential step toward ending passive-aggressive behaviors. Conflict is an unavoidable part of life, but knowing how to assert your feelings effectively can result in better resolutions.

Passive-aggressive behavior can be destructive, but the chances are that we all respond in such ways at times. By understanding what causes such actions and how to deal with them, you can minimize the potential damage to your relationships.

INFORMATION HOARDING

When many people think of hoarding, the first thing that comes to mind is the TV show where houses are packed full of stuff. People can't easily find things that are important to them – and most of the time, they don't even know what is really under the piles that have built up over the years.

While most companies don't have issues with piles of trash and clothes, many do have a hoarding problem – but instead of things, employees are hoarding information.

Employees hoard information in the workplace for a variety of reasons. After years of hard work, employees often become territorial of their knowledge. They fear that sharing information they worked to gain will undermine their expertise, or worse, give credit to others where credit is not due. Some employees hoard information because they feel a sense of job security when others consistently come to them for advice. And in some cases, information sharing and collaboration is not encouraged. But whatever the case may be, the results remain the same; productivity suffers — big time.

Why Does Information Hoarding Occur?

Employees hoard information in the workplace for a variety of reasons. After years of hard work, employees often become territorial of their knowledge. They fear that sharing information they worked to gain will undermine their expertise, or worse, give credit to others where credit is not due. Some employees hoard information because they feel a sense of job security when others consistently come to them for advice. And in some cases, information sharing and collaboration is not encouraged.

But whatever the case may be, the results remain the same; productivity suffers.

Signs of Information Hoarding

The same people are continually answering the same questions.
While it is nice to have your go-to experts, if a handful of folks are continually answering the same questions, it's probably time for a shift. Documenting answers to frequently asked questions in a knowledge-sharing solution gives everyone easy, searchable access to the information. It also provides a platform for input and collaboration around the best answers in specific cases. This means more consistency for your employees, and more time for your top performers to focus on new initiatives.

You are forced to reinvent the wheel when you're putting together presentations.
Does it feel like Groundhog Day every time you pull together information for a presentation? Now, exactly where did I find that image last time? Where is that intro paragraph I used last week?

Imagine a world where everything is cataloged into one central location — a world where the most commonly used and approved information is searchable. When knowledge is accessible to all, you won't waste any time reinventing the wheel (or reinventing the presentation you put together last week).

You lose institutional knowledge when employees leave.
Every company has a couple of these folks. They often take on a mayoral role within your organization. They are well versed in everything from company history to how and why decisions were made in the past to customer examples and anecdotes. The problem is that this information is undocumented and lives in the minds of a handful of people. And without a system in place to retain the knowledge of these employees as they leave or retire, you risk losing some of your most valuable institutional knowledge.

It's essential to not only encourage these employees to share what they know – which many will in a heartbeat – but also promote documentation in an open forum so everyone present and future can access and learn from it.

Answers and files live on individual laptops and in emails.

"I've got it right here. I'll email it to you." How often do you hear this? Does your company's most frequently used files sit in folders on desktops? Not only is this inefficient, but it is hard to keep up-to-date when individual files are spread throughout the organization.

If documents are instead stored in a knowledge-sharing platform, where all can readily access it, your company can eliminate the silos that occur when information sits on individual hard drives and in email inboxes.

Transparency is not valued as part of your company culture.

Do you work in an environment that rewards collaboration and information sharing? Do people discuss their failures along with their successes? Or, do you keep everything hush-hush and under wraps until the last minute to avoid input and conflict?

The truth is that while it may make you feel exposed to share your shortcomings along with your wins, the goal of transparency isn't to focus on individual performance. The goal is to learn from the experience of others and use this knowledge to build plans. And leaders in the transparency movement don't just encourage employees to share; they create communities where it is expected and rewarded.

If you recognize any or all of these symptoms, it's time to banish information hoarding from your organization. Creating a culture of collaboration and knowledge sharing won't happen overnight. But it will happen with an attitude of sharing and technology that empowers collaboration.

STALLING YOUR IDEAS

Making a strategic career change. Saving more of your paycheck.

Paying off debt. Setting money or work goals like these is the easy part; keeping up your momentum, so they stick for the long term? That's where the battle begins.

Maybe your pattern is to create a plan of action so sweeping that it ultimately overwhelms you. Or you get sidetracked and bogged down by the daily grind, and you veer off course. Perhaps you know you want to change but aren't sure what the first step should be, so you end up spinning your wheels. However, you get there, when you sense that you're stuck in ritzville, it's frustrating and discouraging.

HOW DO YOU KNOW
WHEN YOU'RE STUCK?

If things aren't moving forward in your life, and you feel isolated, frustrated, as well as physically, mentally, and spiritually exhausted, chances are you're stuck. But if you can't feel it, listen to yourself. If you often repeat phrases like, "I don't know what to do next . . . I tried that once, and it didn't work for me . . . I'm confused . . . I'm overwhelmed . . . I don't know where to start," then you're in a rut. It would help if you got back on the path to the future you want.

Being stalled at work is rough. If you're not feeling momentum at work, everything feels stagnant. [The reason this happens is] the same as in any other area of life: You don't create clear goals as to what you want to get out of your job and where you hope it will take you. Or you do have goals, but you don't monitor them carefully, and before you know it, you veer off track.

WARNING SIGNS THAT YOUR CAREER IS STALLING

You Haven't Re-Established Your Purpose
Leaders often fail to establish a new purpose and direction once they succeed. "When things change, and new people are coming on board, purpose and direction must be modified. Leaders often struggle to tell a coherent narrative, and people start making decisions at odds with culture or value.

A warning sign that you're hitting the purpose stall is when you think you need to hire an outsider to get to the next level — breakthrough by holding a story-creation session with people from all levels of the organization.

Ask, What are we about here?. "Engage teams to rearticulate values and purpose that will be easy to communicate to the ranks and out to multiple stakeholders."

Your Team Isn't Working Together On Goals
After a success, team members can start acting like freelancers, concerned with their departments, and not agreeing on priorities or strategies.

"The single most critical success factor for high-performing teams is having a shared understanding of why the Team exists, what it is trying to accomplish, and how it will work together.

Work through this career stall by holding frequent meetings or off-sites to ensure team alignment. Create team rules of engagement and require team members to hold each other (and you) accountable to them. Be explicit about the culture that ties the Team together.

Your Job Isn't Challenging Enough
Employees are happiest when they're being bestowed challenges

equating to their skill levels. And when the levels to those challenges drop, so do the interest of the employees.

You'll know that your career is beginning to wane when the requirements of your Job don't put your skills to the test.

The cure to this dilemma is to hunt for opportunities that challenge your abilities. This can either be in the form of attending online classes after office hours, taking up and contributing additional responsibilities, or volunteering to work on an external project.

You Aren't Talking To The Right People

Working at a new level can cause leaders not to make good use of their time. If you feel frustrated that people aren't following your orders, or if you're too busy to talk to stakeholders, you're careers in danger.

Push through by creating a stakeholder management plan. Who will you put on your calendar regularly? What kinds of conversations should you be having with them? Concentrate on developing a strategic network, allocating time for people who control your future.

Your Skills Are Too Standard

Given the age that we live in and how computers are omnipresent in just about any field out there, listing "Microsoft Office" as a skill on your resume is just dipping-into-the-cookie-jar-kind of tactic that even a child can pull off. And if you're applying for a tech company while doing this, you can forget about ever getting on board, much less ask for a promotion.

What you would want to do instead is a list of only the most advanced and specialized jobs that help you stand out from the generic group of potential candidates. Get busy probing job listings that require particular skills that are in line with yours and list as many of those as you can on your resume.

You Can't Articulate Your Vision And Motivate People

If you can't seem to energize employees to own the strategy or spring into action to tackle a new initiative, you're at risk of another career stall. Instead of blaming others for their inability to "get" it, reassess your communication skills and think of yourself as the chief explaining officer.

Whenever possible, make communication two-way; achieve true communication, not the mere transmission. Communicate more than you believe is necessary to ensure sufficient understanding and change your style of communication to reach different people.

Your Boss Is Holding Back On Their Promise

Nothing is more beguiling and damaging to an employee's morale than knowing that the promotion your employer promised you after reaching a certain target, was no longer being offered.

If this isn't a certain sign that you're being held back, we don't know what else is.

The perfect example of this is when a company tells you that they are watching your fantastic performance in an important project and that they have a promotion waiting for you upon its completion.

After completing the project, you are told by many that it was great and that there are numerous positive changes ahead for the company just based on your performance. Everything seems to be going your way just fine, and you are excited about your promotion until you are told that no one said anything about a promotion.

After hearing about that, you feel slightly betrayed but still a bit optimistic, knowing that it might take time for the organization to arrange your compensation. So you wait a bit longer only to have much more time pass you by.

At this point, your suspicions and doubts about the company taking advantage of you start escalating further, so you set up a time to speak with your employer to get to the bottom of the problem. If your bosses continue to push the promotion back after contributing more of your services to them or just refused to promote you, it may as well be time for you to look for an alternative company who not only value your skills and services but also deliver their promises right there and then.

You're No Longer Growing

It's one thing to know that your bosses are dragging your skills along the way without rewarding you for it, but if you're not growing simply because you're not making an effort to expand your repertoire with new skills and expertise, then you have no one to blame for that except yourself.

You can't expect to say that you're being held back if you're not making an effort to show your company that you can handle other responsibilities.

So to fix this, make time to look into the skills that are needed in the job that you want and start learning and practicing them.

Whether it involves reading books, attending conferences, taking up online courses or tutorials, it will be more beneficial for you in the long run, especially if you can persuade your company with your new skills.

You're No Longer Getting High-Profile Tasks As You Once Did

Remember the time your supervisors used to offer you a cut of the more significant projects, and now they don't?

If you don't know about it know, you may eventually come to realize that you're slowly losing the opportunities you were promised and that your colleagues are the ones who are cutting. And when that happens, you'll know for a fact that you're going nowhere in the proverbial corporate ladder.

Your supervisor may assume that you're already working at a very high level, and if you aren't getting high-profile assignments, it may be because you're not where you need to be.

So instead, you should start coming up with your reach projects. By coming up with something that is of value to the company, you will not only showcase what you can do with your current skill set but also what you are capable of accomplishing in the future.

Your Authority Is Waning

Once you've achieved success, you need to keep performing at a high level to maintain your Team's respect. If you give people direction, but they don't follow through, or you start getting passed over for promotion, you may have hit a career stall.

"Shift your actions and behaviors to come across to followers in a more authentically and emotionally. Empathy works and builds character.

Accept a position on the board of a nonprofit, for example, take a community leadership role, or be more involved in your industry.

You Feel Exhausted And Overwhelmed

Once you're operating at a new level, it can be easy to lose sight of your focus. The danger signs of a career stall here are feeling exhausted and overwhelmed, and less energetic and passionate about what you're doing and its impact.

Decide which tasks to do, which to delegate, and which to drop. Allocate your time as if you're going to 'make history. Enforce, with the help of an accountability partner, rational percentages of time on your calendar to the leadership work that matters most.

You've Abandoned Leadership Development

A successful leader's Job is to be a leader of leaders. If you're unsure of your current leadership team and are starting to no longer trust their capabilities, you could be about to hit a career stall.

Take command of shaping your organization's leadership development programs and play a meaningful role in leading them. Commit to becoming a coach as well as a boss, and dedicate discrete-time for both.

While every stall is different, every leader will stall at some point. They might not hit all of them and not all at once. When you're in a meeting where you are the decision-maker, but everybody else has more information at hand, you're at risk. It should be an epiphany that it's you and your behavior that needs to be changed.

You're Not Networking

Getting ahead in a company involves talking to the right people, which also consists of having them know about you.

This involves networking with both the people of your company and those outside of it. Use the extra time other than the one you invest in your daily responsibilities to get to know the people around you.

Learn whatever you can about them and ask if they need any assistance on what they're doing. Establish relationships with those people along the way so that when the time finally comes for that long-awaited promotion, they will be able to recognize your name when they get ahold of your resume.

You Don't Want To Get Better

This problem could be a mix of more than one factor. If your career is being stalled because you don't want to take on new challenges for yourself that can help you advance further up the ladder, something much deeper must be involved.

Your career stalling is simply a matter of motivation.

It is always better to look for new ways to do your Job better and look for something new to do as well. This usually means learning more and trying to keep up with new things.

Nobody wants to be laid back in what they do and keep themselves from getting better at what they are already good at.

You're Passive

Sometimes you can't get ahead in your career because no one in the company knows that you want to. You did not make an effort to get out of your comfort zone and ask for a promotion, a pay bump, or anything else.

Don't just wait for the promotion or raise to fall into your lap, especially if your company keeps track of more than one employee, task, or project.

Being patient and wanting to prove yourself in the beginning stages is one thing, but it's never a good idea to just sit back and wait for something to happen when things aren't going anywhere. Don't hesitate to let your boss know that you want to move up. Many, if not all, companies want their employees to better themselves, even if it helps moves the company's overall level of production up just a bit.

You Hate Your Work

Yes, there are times when we seriously question, "What am I doing here?" If you're not at all engaged with what you're doing or passionate about it, then there is no hope of you getting ahead in your career.

And if that's the kind of mentality that always comes to mind whenever you go to work, then there's no other solution but walking of the company or thinking long and hard about a career change.

Or if you feel like it, you could pinpoint the parts of your job that you like and those you loathe. Perhaps there is a related area that is more to your liking. Try seeing if it's possible to shift your job responsibilities. Otherwise, you should think about getting a new line of work.

Your Performance Is Deteriorating

Not improving at your Job is another reason your career is where it is still. It's just common sense. If your performance hasn't changed in the last year or so, then why would your employer even bother to promote you? You may choose to keep the status quo if you're alright with it, but it's not going to get you ahead in your company.

Look for ways where you can improve the performance of your Job. But don't overcommit to work daily or keep yourself from taking a vacation. All you have to do is focus on the areas where you're already good at and magnify your performance around those.

You Focus Too Much On Yourself

Keep in mind that the most successful executives around the world are team players, so if you also want to acquire that position, then you have to be one yourself.

It's time to stop focusing on how you can get ahead and leave everyone else out in the dust when you should be focusing on helping your team reach its goal.

COMMON BEHAVIORS
GUARANTEED TO STALL
YOUR CAREER

Doing your job well. Fulfilling your job description is no longer enough to make you stand out, even if you perform exceptionally well. Indeed indispensable contributors can rise to the 30,000-foot level and see how their job supports the overall strategy of the organization. Example: Sandy's job description calls for her, as a receptionist, to answer the phone on the second ring, route calls politely and efficiently, greet guests courteously and professionally, and generally create good impressions for anyone calling or visiting the company. That all sounds good, but if Sandy understands that the company's strategy is to grow through increased sales profitably, she will be on the alert for that prospective customer who wants to talk to his sales rep, Janet, who is on vacation. When the prospect calls with an urgent question about the big proposal Janet sent out just before leaving for the Bahamas, Sandy will NOT politely and efficiently send this call to voicemail! Instead, she will get someone from sales to deal with the call immediately, thereby increasing the chances of winning the deal. Can you do your job in ways that are more supportive of company strategy?

Keeping your boss happy. This career tactic worked well for a long time. Not any more. You now need to please your boss's boss. If nobody above your direct supervisor can see your exceptional value, you are less likely to get a raise, bonus, or promotion. It would help if you pushed your value up to a place in the org chart where leaders know how important it is to recognize and reward star performers. True story: Trey worked in the office of a construction company and noticed that through a series of accounting errors, the company was losing over $150,000 per year in profits. He came up with a no-brainer plan to capture that lost value, and eagerly proposed it to his boss. Trey was shocked when the response was, "You weren't hired to worry about that stuff. Just do what I tell you to do and let the owners worry about the bottom line." Trey dutifully obeyed and remained silent about his great idea—until his boss's boss came into the office the next week, and Trey mentioned his proposal. "This is exactly what we want all employees to be thinking about," said the higher-up in response to the plan. The proposal was quickly implemented, and Trey was the only employee to get a bonus that year. Your relationship with your boss is essential, but you owe your loyalty to the company.

Satisfying all customer demands. The customer is always right. Wrong! Customer requests should not be blindly granted in all cases. When customers want you to do things that would violate the mission of the organization, you may have to refuse. A classic example of prioritizing mission over a customer was when Herb Kelleher, head of Southwest Airlines, wrote a letter to a disgruntled passenger who took offense at the humorous manner in which an attendant had recited the pre-flight safety instructions. In response, Mr. Kelleher wrote, "Dear Ms. [customer name]. We'll miss you." He was unwilling to satisfy this customer (or any like her) at the expense of the company's legendary quest for fun. Go, Herb!
Another legitimate reason to disappoint a customer comes from keeping an eye on your competition. For instance, if a customer is demanding a lower price, but all of your competitors are higher priced than your company, the answer should be "no." Even if your price is not the lowest, but your overall value is superior to the competition, "sorry, but no."

Being sensitive to workplace politics. There is nothing quite as tantalizing, entertaining, or captivating as the many dramatic human interactions we can observe at work. Two rules: 1) Be aware of them; and, 2) Don't get pulled into them. Political intrigue almost always divides people into opposing camps. You run the risk of alienating up to half of your colleagues when you side with one individual over another. Remaining aware but aloof will allow you to stay undamaged by power-struggle outcomes no matter which way they go.

Arriving early and leaving late. This is the perfect way to work harder, not smarter. Good luck with that. Hours don't equal results, and burnout won't get you promoted.

Appearing busy and engaged at all times. Yeah, and while you're at it, why don't you eat lunch at your desk so you can look like you're getting even more work done. Don't stop there—you can multitask by conferencing with your boss via Skype in the bathroom on your smartphone! *Dumb* idea! Looking busy and getting things done are two very different things, and your superiors will soon find out which one you've been doing. All they have to do is watch your business results.

Becoming "visible" by piggybacking onto others' successes. Part of being a team player is helping others accomplish essential tasks, but to fast track your career, you also need to become a lightning rod that attracts the hard work and participation of others. If done right, this will make them want to gain visibility by piggybacking onto *your* successes, because you'll be helping them thrive within your network. How do you do this? By sharing the credit with them. Become a leader in adding value to the organization, and others (maybe even your boss) will eagerly follow.

Always volunteering for projects. I can't think of any practice that will suck the life out of you faster than this one. There seems to be an endless number of projects seeking volunteers at any given time. Your mission, if you're wise enough to accept it, is to seek out those projects that are critical to the mission and strategy of the company, and be the first to volunteer for *those*. Do this, and you can even work on fewer initiatives while adding more indispensable value to the organization. This is the secret to working less and getting recognized more.

Dressing like a winner. Yes, you should get dressed before coming to work! And, yes, you should dress well, and look the part if you're hoping for a promotion. No disagreement there. The problem comes when people rely heavily on their appearance as a substitute for actual bottom-line value. There is no substitute for real value, and you were hired to produce it.

Going the extra mile. This could land you precisely one mile farther in the wrong direction if what you're doing is not essential to the strategy of the organization. There is nothing so useless as doing efficiently that which should not be done at all.

MANEUVERING BEHAVIORS

Every workplace has its share of "office politics." It's a source of stress and anxiety and can even interfere with your productivity. Many internships and temporary jobs through the years taught me a lot about how to stay positive in the workplace.

TIPS FOR MANEUVERING
WORKPLACE POLITICS

Be Careful with Social Media
Going beyond the usual warnings about appropriate posts, exercise caution on whom you befriend from work. Make it a general rule not to accept social media requests from coworkers. It's challenging, especially if you are new and want to be on good terms with everyone. However, you'll avoid that awkward moment of explaining why you unfriended someone. Some platforms like LinkedIn are smarter option, but don't feel pressured to accept every invitation. That doesn't mean you shouldn't try to make friends at work. Friends are always a good thing! But take some time to study your peers and determine their character first.

Don't Add to the Gossip Mill
Don't gossip. It seems that people struggle here, but it goes a long way in establishing yourself as a trustworthy and honorable employee. Unfortunately, you may not accumulate many "friends," but remember an office is primarily a place of work. Sitting quietly in the room while coworkers talk about others is also something you shouldn't do. It amounts to complicity with what's happening. Remove yourself or, better yet, stand up for that coworker. It's your responsibility to support a healthy work environment where people are safe from harassment.

Try Something New Every Month
You enjoy having lunch with friends at work, but make it a point to step outside of your comfort zone. Have a personal goal of learning something new about your workplace. For the first month, you might email your supervisor and a manager in the sales department to ask if you can shadow one of the sales associ-

ates for an hour.

What initiatives are they developing, or which platforms do they prefer to use? You may already receive some of the information in a company newsletter or monthly meeting with your manager, but learning about it on-site is a different experience. It's also a great way to establish new working relationships and friendships across departments and even recruit another player for your summer kickball team.

Your Supervisor is your Best Ally

I'm always perplexed when people shy away from their supervisors, perpetuating the "us versus them" mentality. Instead of this avoidance tactic, it's better to maintain a positive relationship with your director or supervisor. Today is a good time to start. Start small by catching him or her by the coffee pot in the morning for a brief conversation. Drop by his or her office now and then with updates about your project. Highlight the contribution of a teammate who provided the creative idea bringing you closer to the project goal! If you work remotely or in another complex, set up times to check in over the phone.

A good supervisor appreciates these efforts. Not all the news may be good, but you've laid the groundwork for productive and constructive conversations. It also sets a record of information that can be used on your annual performance reviews (instead of hearsay).

Know When to Move On

Sometimes a job doesn't turn out to be as promising as you expected. That's part of life. Hopefully, you'll still be able to pull out positive experiences from your time at a company: learning new skills, receiving an award, or increasing efficiency. Uncomfortable work environments, though taxing, still allow you to develop as a professional. What matters is that you came out of it and landed a new position elsewhere with your integrity intact.

IDENTIFYING POLITICAL BEHAVIOR IN AN ORGANIZATION

Political behavior in the workplace as engaging in behind-the-scenes maneuvers to achieve a personal goal within the organization. Workplace politics can make or break your career.

"An example of positive political behavior is identifying and aligning yourself with key influencers to leverage their influence for career development without compromising your values or that of the organization. Negative political behavior is the opposite. It is playing dirty at the expense of someone else – for example, watching a colleague make a mistake on a project and then turning around to report them to your boss and offering to correct the error."

If workplace politics are dividing your organization, it is essential to take notice and identify the root cause. There are several warning signs that your organization may need some structural changes.

Signs of a politicized business environment:

1. An individual's rewards do not align with organizational rewards.
2. There is a "system" that needs to be worked, and the best navigators are rewarded.
3. Urgency takes a back seat to process, and the stakeholders in the status quo become threatened by change.
4. People who do not regularly produce results don't get fired or reprimanded.
5. The average employee has little knowledge of and visibility into the company's decision-making.

Other indicators of negative office politics include a perceived distance between lower-level employees and executives, closed-door meetings with exclusive information that isn't discussed with the rest of the organization, and star employees leaving because they don't see a path to advancement.

HOW TO AVOID WORKPLACE POLITICS IN YOUR ORGANIZATION

Minimizing politics in a growing organization begins with its leadership, and the best way to accomplish this goal is to encourage transparency and collaboration among team members at all levels. Frankel advised taking the following steps to break down the divisive walls of negative politics at work.

Reduce distance from company decisions.
As small companies grow and add more structure, policies, and management layers, the average employee naturally becomes further removed from executive leadership on a day-to-day basis. Management teams need to be mindful that this distance from company decisions is a key factor in politics, infiltrating even the most successful companies.
Promote communication and transparency among teams by holding regular meetings, town halls, and group lunches. Make sure everyone knows what the corporate objectives are, and talk openly and honestly about the challenges the company is facing. Trust all employees (not just executives and managers) with information and make them stakeholders in the success of the company. When leaders trust their team and empower them with insights into company challenges, the team can take an active part in conquering those challenges.

Don't tolerate political behavior.
Everyone's success should be measured, first and foremost, by the overall company objectives. When even the hint of "me first" behavior crops up in a meeting or email, ensure it gets squashed

swiftly. The pushing of personal agendas, no matter who participates in it or at what level of the organization, should not be rewarded. The minute leadership accepts political or bureaucratic behavior; it is an invitation for it to run rampant within the company culture.

Demand accountability from all team members.

Each employee should understand their role and how it contributes to the success of the company, and then be expected to deliver. When the company has a big success or reaches a milestone, it should be recognized both as a team win and a celebration of the success of those whose work contributed to it at all levels of the organization – not just the senior salesperson, head engineer or manager.

Likewise, when a mistake or failure occurs, those who contributed to it should be expected to take ownership of their roles (and that includes executive management) so that the mistake can be fixed and not occur again. When employees are willing to be praised for the wins but afraid to take responsibility for the losses, it shows they are more interested in their success than the companies.

"No matter how committed a leader is, the work environment cannot be completely depoliticized. However, executives that make a concerted effort to [be more accessible and transparent] can effectively reduce the impact that politics will have as an obstacle to the company's success."

HOW TO DEAL WITH
OFFICE POLITICS

Make friends

To fix a toxic work culture, you need to get involved. When people feel they don't belong in a group, their physical health and wellbeing plummet – so, if you're feeling isolated or excluded by negative office politics, it makes sense to try to make friends.

If one person at work is the primary source of conflict, the best way to deal with them is to unite with your co-workers. Grouping against a bully will provide victims with support for their feelings since victims of bullies are at risk of becoming isolated. Through joining together and discussing the bully's behavior, co-workers can contain the bully, who, with their behavior exposed, loses the power to terrorize – and faces the threat of isolation."

This strategy also works with game-playing colleagues – people with bullying tendencies often try to isolate victims, so the more people you have on your side, the less likely you are to be taken advantage of at work.

Document your time

When you are subject to colleagues' political tactics – such as taking credit for your work – it's important not to retaliate. "It's tempting to expose the co-worker or boss in front of others, but this can backfire.

It would help if you were smarter than that: "Make sure you document your work thoroughly and let co-workers and your bosses' superiors know what you are doing and have done. This protects your reputation: if your work ethic is called into question by colleagues, you then have a way to prove your productivity.

Don't sink to their level

When colleagues try to make you look bad or undermine you, it's tempting to do likewise. However, this can backfire: you may come across as petty and is unlikely to change your boss or co-worker's behavior.

A better way to deal with difficult colleagues is to ask them for a private conversation. Calmly ask them why they acted how they did, rather than accusing them. This is often the best way to change behavior, as it requires them to reflect on their actions.

Change the culture from within

Office politics should be looked at as something that can be re-framed into a positive. It would help if you worked to contribute to the culture at your company that values people and discourages abusing people in any form.

The best way to do this is to praise others, encourage teamwork, and be empathetic to your co-workers. By making an effort to change the culture to one of kindness and honesty, you can create a better environment for everyone.

Go it alone

For some people, the effort of attempting to navigate and even change poor office politics is too much of an uphill battle. If you try the tips above and still find your office a nightmare, there is a more straightforward option: ditch the co-workers entirely by working for yourself.

JOCKEYING THE POSITION

Jockey for the position is the act of competing against others for a desirable role or thing.

To try to come out ahead in a competition for something specific or put oneself in a more favorable position generally.

If someone jockeys for position, they try to get into a better position or situation than people they are competing against.

HOW TO DEAL WITH COMPETITION AT WORKPLACE

Assess the Situation

First things first, you need to assess the situation and make sure there aren't any misunderstandings. The more you get to know your colleague, the more you'll figure out about their personality and how they work. You can then detect if they are, in fact, the opposite.

Don't Lose Focus

It's easy to let a competitive coworker become the existence of your work life, deliberately making you lose Focus on your actual work – and creating an easy win for them. So, learn to fight the temptation and stay focused on what you were employed to do.

Form Alliances

If a specific colleague is trying to throw everyone under the bus, it's time you joined forces to take the troublemaker down. Let people know that you can be trusted and that you're a team player. For example, if you see someone is inching closer to a deadline and still has a lot of work to do, offer them your help (as long as your workload can be pushed to the side for another day, of course).

Be Competitive with Yourself

Use this unhealthy competition to better yourself and your skills, and generally shift the energy to focus on improving your strengths and weaknesses in the workplace. Competitive people get things done and have much self-discipline, perseverance, and stamina, typically not giving up quickly in the pursuit to be the best at whatever they are aiming for. Because competitive people are frequently very motivated and perform at a high level, they can often inspire others to function and perform to the best of their abilities as well'.

Talk to Your Boss

Having an open conversation with your manager may be the only resolution to this unhealthy environment. It's important to tread carefully when approaching this situation, though, as you won't want to look like you're causing conflict in the office. A great way to start the conversation is: 'There's someone in the office whose attitude is negatively affecting team morale and productivity. What do you think is the best way to handle this?' Just make sure you have evidence to support your claims. Otherwise, it's your word against theirs!

Don't Bite Back

No matter how much the competitor tries to provoke you, it's imperative that you bite the bullet and don't answer back. Their behavior may be the result of insecurities, and if that's the case, they probably feel threatened by your success and will exhaust all avenues to try and shed you in a bad light. Make sure you're always civil and respectful to everyone in the workplace – even if you secretly dislike them!

Be Likeable

The hypercompetitive colleague you're dealing with may be intimidated by you and may think you'll try to sabotage their successes and will often automatically mark you as the enemy before they even get to know you. To combat this, do your best to show them that that just isn't you and be genuinely friendly with them.

Compliment Them

Flattery may be the way to win over your rival and get them to see that you're not a threat. As I explained earlier, many people are often competitive as they are insecure, and if you help boost their ego, they'll most likely drop the act and be friendlier towards you.

Keep Your Distance

By staying out of their way, you'll be much happier in the workplace. Try to avoid them as much as possible, and don't engage in any conversation with them to ensure you remain as calm as possible.

Correspond in Writing

Following on from the previous point, if you do have to engage in any work-related conversation with them, make sure it's all through writing, whether it's via email or on your company's chat system. Be sure to keep copies of your communication in case it's needed in the future. It's always best to keep a mutual party to ensure you're receiving all the information that you need to proceed with your task.

Ask to Move Teams

If you really can't see eye-to-eye with your competitive colleague, consider moving teams or departments if possible. There's no guarantee that the grass will be greener on the other side, but if you're that unhappy, you might as well try.

Speak Up in Meetings

If you notice that a particular colleague is stealing your ideas and suggesting them in team meetings, speak up about it! You could say something like: "Thank you for sharing the idea that I mentioned earlier, Jane... I think it will be..." and then continue to elaborate on your thought process behind it.

Stay in the Loop

If there's any gossip circulating the office about you, you'll want to know about it. So, although I usually advise against getting involved in office politics, in this case, you'll need to keep one ear open to know if your competitor is spreading any unfounded and hurtful rumors about you.

Know Your Rights

If your colleague is using deceptive and unfair methods to compete against you (for example, they are abusing the system and taking your good leads to be at the top of the game' and win the end-of-month bonus), file a complaint and report what's going on to your HR department who will be able to investigate the matter further.

Try Working with Them

As the saying goes: 'if you can't beat them, join them.' In this instance, you can try working with your colleagues and asking for their advice while you're at it. It might help them see that you're not a rival and that there's no need for animosity.

Act with Integrity

Regardless of how your competitive colleagues choose to act, avoid engaging in any petty competition and always to use morally right means in all your endeavors.

84% of business leaders (including corporate recruiters) believe integrity to be the essential quality in an employee. In other words, be the star employee that you are, and let your jealous coworker continue digging themselves a bigger hole.

Find Another Job

If you have exhausted all your options and you're still feeling the effects of a toxic work environment, it might be time for you to look elsewhere for another job. You need to think about your happiness, and if you really can't resolve your differences with your annoying colleague, then you'll need to find an escape route.

MASTERING THE OFFICE COMPETITION AND POLITICS

We've all heard that life isn't a competition, but let's face it, does anyone believe that? It might be something we tell children alongside tales about Santa Claus, but we all know who's leaving presents under the tree. Competition in the workplace is inevitable, and in fact, valuable. Where would Ali have been without Frazier? The Beatles without the Rolling Stones? Pac-Man without Blinky, Pinky, Inky, and Clyde?

Healthy competition pushes us to excel, to take chances, and to better ourselves. Of course, competition has its toxic dark side: it can drain your morale, blind you to organizational goals, and exacerbate stress. The key to winning lies in competing on your terms, taking advantage of your strengths, and making the most of your opportunities.

Focus on yourself

The reality is that no matter where you work, you're going to encounter individuals who are more capable and successful. Colleagues will be promoted ahead of you, maybe get larger bonuses. But it's critical to remember that you were hired for a reason and that you possess abilities and skills that your employers value. Instead of focusing on a colleague's career path, work to understand your unique strengths, and identify opportunities that will help showcase your talents.

If you feel insecure about your abilities for any reason, be brave, and identify its source. Maybe you could use more training or professional and personal development to build your confidence and assuage lingering doubts about your skill set.

Identify individuals whose career paths mirror your aspirations and learn from them. What have they done to achieve their successes? What insight could they provide to you?

Forge alliances

Competition can be brutal, but you don't have to struggle alone. Everyone needs help in the workplace. Reach out to individuals in other departments and groups regularly to create opportunities for collaboration and mutual support. It's crucial to build up a deep internal network of allies whom you can support and who can do the same for you. When working with others, be clear about what you need and listen to your colleagues so that you have a deep understanding of their needs and how you can support them. In meetings, use inclusive language. Instead of saying "I," say "We" when you're discussing projects, teamwork, and objectives. After all, everyone is committed to working towards success.

And, just like Luke needed his Yoda, having a mentor and a sponsor in a competitive environment can be a huge asset. Most successful individuals will mention how a mentor inspired and guided them. Their experience, insight, and perspective mean that there will be chances for you to learn from someone else's mistakes and not your own for once. A sponsor can be your internal advocate, someone who will help advance your cause and who can speak on your behalf, providing you with exposure and projects that will stretch and test your abilities.

Work with, and not against, the competition

Overly competitive individuals abound in workplaces, and dealing with them can be difficult, but there are ways to cope.

Talk to them and be polite and civil. A signal to overly competitive colleagues that you are not a threat may motivate them to treat you nicely in return. It can also help to ask them for insight and advice about the work they do; praise them too for work that's done well. Flattery goes a long way, and who knows? They might embrace you as someone they can trust.

Watch your back

Of course, a different approach is justified when you're forced to deal with colleagues who actively seek to undermine you. You know the type. They're saboteurs. He or she's the one who "forgot" to invite you to a meeting or to copy you on an important email, who takes credit for your work and who neglects to acknowledge your contributions. With these individuals, you'd better watch your back.

Document your contributions in detail and maintain copies of everything you do, especially as it relates to any work involving the problematic colleague. Update your manager regularly on the work you've been doing. In the highly likely event that your coworker attempts to throw you under the bus to explain away their own mistakes or paint you in a less than flattering light, you'll have documented and verifiable evidence to refute any claims.

If you suspect your coworker of snooping, deploy passwords to protect any electronic files you use at the office and keep your desk and any storage areas locked with a key. Chances are your competitor will attempt to pry information out of you by acting friendly, so it's best to be wary and minimize contact with them as much as possible. If you do have to engage in a conversation, be professional and respectful, but maintain your distance.

Finally, let such colleagues know that you're aware of what they're doing. Call them out on their tactics and show them that you're far from an easy target. However, a confrontation might not be something with which you're entirely comfortable. In that case, please speak with your manager and let him or her know what's happening and how this individual's behavior is influencing your performance and satisfaction, and what you've done to resolve the issue.

Life is a competition, but it can often encourage us to perform beyond even our potentials and expectations. The key to surviving workplace competition is to ensure that it stays healthy by balancing it with a deep sense of mutual respect for your colleagues, and a recognition that you're all bound by a common desire: to perform well and succeed.

Overall, the best way to deal with a competitive coworker is to avoid sinking to their level. Stay true to yourself and make sure you focus on your work and career goals.

WAYS TO TAKE DOWN A HYPER-COMPETITIVE COWORKER

Maintain Focus

Don't let an overly competitive coworker draw your attention away from your job. Focus on doing solid work and continuously improving – not on besting a particular colleague. Put: Don't compete – except against yourself. Use your past performance to set future goals and work towards those results. You're more likely to succeed if you focus on the positive goal of continual self-improvement, rather than on outdoing someone else.

Cultivate Relationships

Work to build and maintain strong, professional relationships with other colleagues. Again, don't focus on the overly competitive coworker. Instead, put energy into gaining respect in the workplace and becoming a well-regarded and valuable member of the team overall: Deliver on commitments; praise others; accept constructive criticism; collaborate well, and be a positive presence. Work toward virtuous goals and leave the negativity of the hyper-competitive coworker behind.

Convert

Try to get an overly competitive coworker to start viewing you more as a collaborator than a rival. When the coworker in question does something well, casually recognize it during a meeting with a quick compliment. Ask for his advice on a project you're working on – and if he provides a useful suggestion, give him credit when appropriate. If you try these methods, however, and he isn't receptive, leave it alone. Maybe he's too far gone into his competitiveness.

Defend Yourself

Sometimes taking steps, such as those mentioned above, to neutralize an overly competitive coworker aren't enough. Blatant attacks against you or your work – and attempts to steal ideas and credit from you – must be answered. Before you go to the boss, however, be sure that the violation is severe enough to warrant such action. You don't want to be a tattletale. And when you do talk to your boss, keep it professional, be specific, and be able to support your position. Don't get personal; don't whine, and don't gripe.

Evaluate Culture

Take a look at your workplace. How many of your colleagues would you describe as overly competitive? If the number is high, there may be more significant forces at work. An abundance of hyper-competitive coworkers could be an indication that there is a workplace culture — either encouraged or ignored by those in charge — that creates and fosters that behavior. If that's the case, and you are unhappy with the situation, it may be time to think about looking for a new job with a company that has a culture more appealing to you.

ALLIANCE BUILDING

An ally is an associate who assists and often, friendship. Your partners are likely to support your views and causes. They help solve problems, provide advice, act as a sounding board when you need a listening ear, and offer a different perspective so you can view your organization more broadly.

Allies are people who offer one another backing, assistance, advice, information, protection, and even friendship. They go the extra mile to help out.

Strong and mutually beneficial alliances can help each party to survive and to thrive, and to get things done more quickly and smoothly than if they were to go it alone.

For example, if you're behind schedule and about to miss an important deadline, you could avoid damaging your reputation, or that of your organization, if you had allies to call on to lend a hand.

And knowing that there are people who've "got your back" can reduce stress, boost your confidence and resilience, and encourage rapport and collaboration.

BENEFICIAL WAYS OF BUILDING ALLIANCES AT WORK

"Networking" isn't icky.
Some of you are cringing. The notion of "making friends" with conscious awareness of your ability to help one another makes some people uncomfortable. The secret of success is sincerity. Once you can fake that, you've got it made."

But it doesn't work that way. When you are genuinely interested in someone else (either one-on-one or as part of a team effort), it feels good to make friends. The only difference is that, in this case, friendship also includes enlightened self-interest.

"If you develop a personal connection, empathy, and understanding with another person, they are more likely to help you, despite everything else they have on their plate. When you're friends (or at least allies) with work colleagues, they know that you understand their world, and they appreciate that you would adequately and appropriately represent their needs as you move your project forward. They knew I had, or would, do the same for them when needed."

Build a culture of helping others
I like to think that, in most companies, it's not that unusual for people to want to help each other, even when they work in wholly different departments. The company is supposed to share the same values, after all, and most of us are nice people. You (and the managers who provide the corporate vision) should build a company culture in which it is expected that team members will help each other out of a jam.

When you do get that kind of "We're in it together" group behavior, the attitude becomes part of the tribal belief system and is reinforced by peer pressure. If you're lucky enough for team members to have a tacit understanding of their shared goals, it's far easier to create people-connections that – to use the in-buzz-words, though here I mean them explicitly – foster collaboration, build trust, and make people feel safe enough to share aloud a "dumb" (but innovative) idea.

As a general rule, you should be responsive ahead of time. Treat other people in the company with respect and help them if they need it, within reason. Establish a reputation as a helpful person on a useful team. Coworkers are more inclined to help when the culture of your team is to help others.

But... maybe your situation is far from ideal. How do you build these alliances across the business? Here are a few things that might help.

Number One with a bullet: Offer help.

Want to earn someone's affection? Make his life more comfortable. The people I know who are most-beloved and best-connected are all generous with their time and attention. Nor do they wait to be asked: They all offer to help the people they know, even acquaintances.

I don't mean to say that you need to volunteer to take on a huge project for somebody you barely know. In most cases, it's just a matter of learning what matters to the individual and letting her know about an item of interest.

What's important is that you do something to help your colleagues with *their* needs, long before you need to ask for help with your own. "Sometimes it's a listening ear; sometimes it's 'roll up your sleeves' and help them get their deliverables done. They need to know that you're not thinking of them as a cog in a machine, that you think of them as a person who matters. That shouldn't be any great difficulty. After all, your colleague *is* a person who matters – and helping good people is always rewarding on its own merits.

Express appreciation

Breaking news: People like to feel valued and appreciated.

But somehow, people rarely take a moment to say Attagirl, as if offering colleague praise is more dangerous than criticizing. Gosh, what's wrong with saying you noticed that someone did an excellent job – mainly when it's obvious that they put heart and soul into it?

Many of us are so focused on doing our jobs with a precision that we look first at the errors (our own, not just those emanating from the Accounting department or Marketing), and we put our attention on the correction. Or we assume, "It's just their job!" and (like this scene from Mad Men) the paycheck should be all the Thank-You someone needs.

But even though we know *we* respond best when people tell us we did well, we often are reluctant to say so to others. I'm not sure why that is.

If you want to build relationships with people across your company, take a moment to say Thank You. Don't wait for your colleague to do something exceptional. Right now, *yes,* write an email message to someone in another department, saying something like, "I was thinking today about how often I drop a request on you out of the blue, and how cheerfully and quickly you always respond. Like [recent example]. I may not always remember to say Thank You, but I want you to know that I noticed and appreciated it."

Three sentences… and it'll make someone's day. It cannot sound insincere because it *is* sincere. And you betcha that, six months from now, if you ask for that colleague's help with your project, she'll be delighted to say Yes – even if she has other demands on her time.

"Flattery gets you nowhere? On the contrary, it works pretty consistently.

Praise publicly

Even more useful: When someone does go out of his way for you, give them public recognition, especially in front of his boss. "Publicly recognize them in either a mention in your project proposal,

Thank You Note to their superiors, and a gift of appreciation. When you create magic moments for others, not only will you feel good, but the people you're coming in contact with will feel good, and it will have a ripple effect."

Eventually, you will need to call upon people in another department to help you out when your need is a distraction from their jobs. In that case, the other person has to want to help you. By following a few of these suggestions – which makes the office a friendlier place no matter what! – you might find it easier to get that help when you need it.

Take advantage of group outings
Whether your company hosts a weekly happy hour, optional town-hall-style meetings, or posts open positions for its softball team, you should say "yes" more often than "no" to these invitations to make new work friends. That's because these scenarios pull you out of your work bubble and can connect you with people in many different departments. This is a perfect opportunity to learn more about your company but also find friends across the company."

Resist gossiping
Gabbing about the weird poster Anne has pinned to her cubicle. At the same time, you're at the communal coffee spot may seem like a good ice breaker, but participating in or worse, initiating office gossip can stunt the growth of work relationships.

"Be cautious not to spread rumors or gossip, because they can spread like wildfire through a workplace. They can poison the environment and reflect badly on you."

Eat-in the communal kitchen
You're surrounded—probably, quite literally—at work. So, who could blame you if your instinct is to grab a solo lunch, or sip your coffee while you hide in the stairwell? "But slow down. Stop by the communal kitchen on your way out and "chit chat with your coworkers—ask them about their day, weekend plans, their fa-

vorite Keurig flavor or lunch spot. "Just get to know them."

Offer to help

If your coworker sends you a message, and wants your advice, take advantage of them reaching out to build a relationship. How so? Instead of replying in kind—whether on any communication channel like slack or via email—offer to set up a face to face meeting so that you can take on the issue together. Then, "remember to insert some chit chat, like, 'Did you watch the new season?' or 'Any vacation plans coming up?'.

Find common ground beyond your cubicles

A big key to making work friends is to talk about things *other* than work. If you can get to know coworkers' interests outside the office, you may find some common ground on which to build a friendship.

Remember: Not all friendships last forever

If you make new friends at work, realize that not each one of them will always be in your corner. "Some workplace friendships do turn sour. "If that happens, you need to remain civil and professional. You don't want to let the breakup interfere with your work or make coworkers feel uncomfortable."

SET UP TO FAIL

Setting up to fail is a phrase denoting a no-win situation designed in such a way that the person in the situation cannot succeed at the task which they have been assigned. It is considered a form of workplace bullying.

There are also situations in which an organization or project is set up to fail and where individuals set themselves up to fail.

The first known documented use of "set up to fail" was in 1969.

HOW TO KNOW IF YOU'RE BEING SET UP TO FAIL AT WORK

Regardless of the task, your manager is always looking over your shoulder. And no matter what you do, it's never good enough.

Some days you even wonder if your boss wants you to quit.

Do you recognize this scenario? If so, you're likely caught up in "set-up-to-fail syndrome." This organizational dynamic was first identified by French academics Jean-Francois Manzoni and Jean-Louis Barsoux in 1998 as part of the research that explored "why seemingly good employees sometimes imploded."

It starts with a good employee, not performing up to par, even just one time. As a result, the boss begins to doubt the employee and often starts to micromanage them.

The employee, in turn, senses this shift and starts to lose confidence in their work. That behavior causes the boss to doubt the employee even more, and lower expectations, causing even more self-doubt and under-performance by the employee — and around and around and down and down it goes."

These situations are not always born of malicious intent. Instead, the boss is merely micromanaging the employee in what they see as an effort to help them. They're usually mystified when their oversight causes performance to worsen. For the employee's part, they're mystified too, because they're so careful and obedient.

And ultimately, they're wondering, "Why isn't the boss happier?" The situation almost invariably ends with the employee departing, on their own volition or not.

If all of this sounds familiar to you, then your best bet is to take action — now. Go above and beyond to show your boss you're an asset they can be sure of.

"Enlarge a small assignment, and nail it. Volunteer for a task no one else wants to embrace every challenge with sunny enthusiasm.

Ultimately, if you want to keep your job and repair your relationship with your manager, you're going to need to stop overthinking the dilemma and muster your confidence and determination to prove yourself anew.

The time for paranoia has passed. The cycle is yours to break.

HOW TO HANDLE BEING SET UP FOR FAILURE AT WORK

Do you have a strong feeling that people or forces are conspiring against you at work? Have you noticed that some of your colleagues withhold information or resources necessary for you to reach your goals? Unfortunately, in a recent BioSpace Community Survey, some life science professionals indicated they felt like they were being set up for failure. A lack of transparency, insignificant decisions, little guidance or feedback is provided, and unrealistic expectations were all mentioned. As a result of a variety of circumstances, many professionals believe that there is no way to meet their performance targets.

It's normal for frustration to set in when you think that you're doing all you can, but forces beyond your control determine your results. If you work for an organization that doesn't prioritize open communication at all employee levels, things can become even more complicated. You might also receive conflicting advice about what you should do in the workplace to change things. Here's how to handle the feeling that you're being set up for failure!

Think ahead
Let's say you've noticed multiple situations, instances, and facts that lead you to believe others are working against you. First, run the details by a trusted colleague, mentor, or coach outside of your organization. They can help to provide an unbiased view of what has happened. If you're sure that you are being set up, it's time to start thinking ahead in regards to your actions. How might your manager and coworkers view your current performance? Telling others within your company about your thoughts

prematurely can do more harm than good. Think about how your future actions will affect your days, weeks, and months down the line.

Create a paper trail

Start collecting evidence of what you suspect is going on. Keeping relevant documents, emails, files, and notes is very important. Creating a paper trail that's physical or electronic will be beneficial if you have to expose what is going on to others. Record a timeline of events to keep for yourself, so you remember specific details. You must be able to distinguish between objective facts and any subjective feelings you may have. Proof of intent and harmful activities would be necessary if you plan to approach internal management or an external attorney.

Do your best work

If you are being sabotaged in some way, the best response is to produce your best work! Going above and beyond what's expected can help others see how valuable you are. This might be difficult to accomplish if someone is making it nearly impossible for you to do your job. Think about any workarounds or alternate solutions to attain the resources and support you need to be successful. This could require some creativity on your part, but think about what new ways you can get things done that don't rely on the status quo. Doing your best work, regardless of the circumstances, also helps to build your leadership skills.

Be open with management or human resources

Depending on how blatant and damaging the attempt to set you up is, you might have to get your boss or manager involved. If you think what is going on could permanently damage your reputation, eliminate your chance of success, and cause you to lose your job, speaking with your manager is vital. Request a one-on-one meeting with your boss and try to divulge as little information as you can before the meeting. During the discussion, tell them what has been going on while emphasizing the facts (as opposed to your subjective feelings). Sharing the paper or electronic trail of events can also be helpful. Afterward, sincerely wait to hear their feedback. You believe your manager is the person working against you; consider being open with someone in your human resources department.

At some point in your career, you might feel as though other professionals are setting you up for failure. Before deciding that is actually what's going on, run the facts by others you trust. If indeed you can conclude aspects of sabotage are at play, think multiple steps ahead when it comes to your actions. Begin creating a paper trail and electronic filing system to keep up with questionable incidents and events. Maintain a positive outlook by focusing on doing your best work. Finally, if things are severe, be open with management and human resources about what's going on in a one-on-one meeting. What can you do to handle a situation like this?

Reframe Your Mindset

Here's a fact: Few managers *want* you to fail. Think about it—what do they have to gain? Unless your manager is who feeds on the failings of others, they stand to lose as much as you do. If a manager wants to push you out by forcing failure upon you, that's a pretty roundabout way of dealing with a personal issue. Most managers don't have time for those games.

Why not shift your mindset and look for another reason you're feeling this way? Is it possible that you're just being challenged? Could it be that your manager gives you the hardest, ugliest, most problematic projects because he or she has faith in your abilities? Is it possible that you've created an impossibly high standard for success, and you're setting *yourself* up to fail?

Try looking at the situation through a different, less personal lens. Most managers want their people to succeed. They might not know precisely how to help make that happen, but it doesn't mean they're actively working against you.

Explain What You Need

Let's work on the assumption that your manager is NOT, in fact, a monster. If you're facing a situation that is doomed to fail, speak up, and tell your manager what resources you need to turn it around. Few things are so hopeless that there's nothing to be done.

Unfortunately, your manager can't read your mind. You have to make direct requests for whatever it is you need, explain why it's necessary, and articulate the consequences if it's not provided.

Reset Expectations

Don't allow yourself to get set up to fail by accepting unrealistic expectations. All too often, people are afraid to push back, and they end up agreeing to impossible things. Whether it's an unrealistic deadline or a predicted result that's straight out of fantasyland, it's your responsibility to rein things in.

Offer an alternative expectation that is achievable and discuss why the adjustment needs to happen. If the original parameters stand, clearly communicate the other changes that will need to occur as a consequence. For example, maybe you will need an extra team member to meet that crazy deadline or a larger budget to achieve those fantastic results. Your job is to play an active role in the expectation-setting process. Do not merely accept that dog-of-a-project without at least attempting to clean it up a bit.

Move On

It's worthwhile noting that some environments make success practically impossible. After all, if you're selling broken watches, you could be the best salesperson in the world, but you're still set up to fail. Whether the problem is caused by management, organizational incompetence, or anything else, you have to ask yourself the hard question: "Is it me or is it them?"

If you're convinced that the situation is irreversible, cut your losses and move on. Working in a situation where you can't win is exhausting and depressing—and it does nothing to advance your career.

CONCLUSION

Political fray

Fray is a fight, struggle, or disagreement that involves many people.

You hate that people consistently show up to meetings late. You find your company's maternity policy woefully inadequate. You think the company's IT system is out of date. It's normal to be bothered by work issues like these, but when do you move from complaining to taking action? How do you decide which battles to fight?

While it is generally a good thing that people are involved in politics and are expressing opinions, it might not be in your best interest to get into a raging argument at work with someone who does not share your views.

Avoiding political frays

You spend many hours of the day at work, so it's inevitable some-one in the office will broadcast their opinion. Unfortunately, this is out of your control. What you *can* control is how you handle the situation.

Here are ways of keeping the argument at bay.

Avoid party politics.

It can be really easy to get sucked into a right versus left debate.

Have employees, instead, discuss big-picture concepts, specific ballot measures, or general concern. Please encourage them to talk about how they would be affected by changes to help explain why they are concerned about specifics.

This way, it is easier to see both sides of the debate, and discus-sions are more likely to be constructive. People can get very fired up when it comes to the identity of the political party they support, so sticking to the facts and issues can help everyone educate each other.

Understand why conflict arises.

It is useful to get to the bottom of why conflict arises. Usually, it comes from people having different objectives, opinions, interpretations of a situation, or views of what is acceptable behavior. "Political discussion is often an emotionally rooted affair, with strong ideological roots, possible immediate impact on family situations, even immediate impact on work situations and living standards.

Be respectful.

Political opinions tend to be a personal matter, so it is essential to treat peoples' views and opinions with respect.

Everyone has a right to believe what they do, and they have their reasons. By treating everyone with the same level of respect, opinions are more likely to be shared without things getting nasty.

You might not understand how a person can have the opinions they do, but the best way of trying is by listening.

"You may not agree with everything they say, but you need to understand that to them, their view is correct and is rooted in inherited and developed life influences that you will probably never understand.

Know when to stop.

It's essential employees understand when they should end a conversation. If a discussion is making someone feel uncomfortable, it's a good idea to move onto something else. Say you respect their point of view and appreciated the talk and change the subject.

Employers should set the boundaries for healthy political debate. If you have individuals in the workplace who are keen political activists have a quiet word to ensure they don't campaign during working hours, wear political slogans and badges in the office and use company equipment and communication tools to voice their party allegiance and garner voters.

It is also worth reminding staff of their responsibilities, especially when speaking to customers and suppliers, as these could align the company in a way it feels is inappropriate.

Don't post anything on social media in anger.

While employees generally aren't prevented from being vocal about things outside of work, some are advised to be careful when putting on any social media platforms.

Pretty much everyone has a smartphone now, and you might have a few of your colleagues on a few social media channels. This means you could quickly get into an online spat that continues into your work life during the week.

Read all content carefully and consider the consequences before expressing personal views on social media, and sharing articles or memes.

Know your place.

It's worth working out where your boss stands on political discussions at work. If your superiors frown on it, then the workplace probably isn't the place for these conversations.

If it's encouraged, debates can be a great way of nurturing respect within the team.

While you need to be aware of the conflicting opinions that can arise from political discussions and how to deal with these, focus on the positives.

If you're in a senior role, your colleagues will naturally be interested in your viewpoint, especially if your opinions on specific policies are work-related.

Only share what you need to share.

Knowledge is power. The more information colleagues have on you, and the more you know about them, the more responsibility you both carry.

For example, if an employee and manager had a heated discussion in the office, then the employee is let go, it could look like they were fired because of their beliefs.

With political issues like immigration and Brexit, there's also the potential for colleagues to overstep the mark. In these cases, make sure any offense is followed up with the appropriate procedure, so there isn't any chance of politically motivated harassment.

Just be careful.

Ultimately, be careful about what you say and when you say it. Political discussion is enlightening and exciting, but it's essential to be able to differentiate between the issues that can spark healthy debates and those which could cause offense. The last thing you want is to create a division in your office.

If people care, that is a positive thing. Provided discussions take place respectfully, and within the boundaries set for the courteous debate, there's no reason why a politically engaged workforce shouldn't be able to remain productive and harmonious.